New
King
James
Version
Edition

40
DAYS

Prayers *and* Devotions to Prepare *for* *the* Second Coming

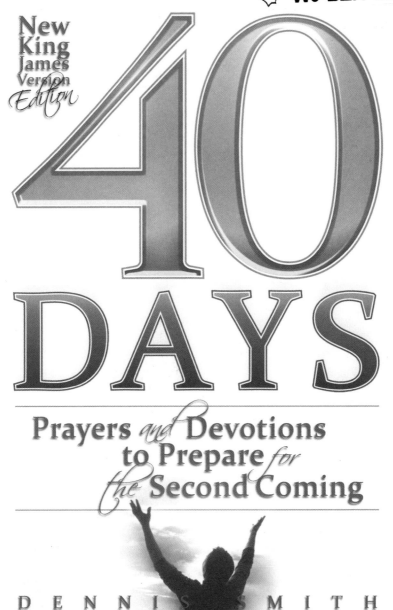

DENNIS SMITH

REVIEW AND HERALD® PUBLISHING ASSOCIATION
Since 1861 | www.reviewandherald.com

Also by Dennis Smith:
40 Days: Prayers and Devotions to Prepare for the Second Coming (KJV Edition)

To order, call **1-800-765-6955**.

Visit us at **www.reviewandherald.com**
for information on other Review and Herald® products.

——————————————————————

Copyright © 2010 by Review and Herald® Publishing Association
Published by Review and Herald® Publishing Association, Hagerstown, MD 21741-1119

Edited by Kalie Kelch
Copyedited by James Hoffer
Cover design by Ron Pride
Interior design by Patricia S. Wegh
Typeset: Times New Roman 11/15

Unless otherwise noted, all Scripture is quoted from the NKJV. Texts credited to NKJV are from the New King James Version. Copyright © 1979, 1980, 1982, by Thomas Nelson, Inc. Used by permission. All rights reserved.

Texts credited to NIV are from the Holy Bible, New International Version. Copyright © 1973, 1978, 1984, International Bible Society. Used by permission of Zondervan Bible Publishers.

PRINTED IN U.S.A.

14 13 12 11 10   5 4 3 2 1

Library of Congress Cataloging-in-Publication Data

Smith, Dennis Edwin, 1944-
   40 days : prayers and devotions to prepare for the Second Coming / Dennis Smith.
      p. cm.
   1. Second Advent—Prayers and devotions. 2. Baptism in the Holy Spirit—Textbooks.
I. Title. II. Title: Forty days.
   BT886.3.S65 2010
   242'.2—dc22
                                2010012486

ISBN 978-0-8280-2544-7

Contents

INTRODUCTION~

Section III: Spirit Baptism and Evangelism

Section IV: Spirit Baptism and Abiding in Christ

Section V: Spirit Baptism and Fellowship

Introduction

This 40-days-of-study-and-prayer devotional is designed to prepare God's church for Christ's second coming, as well as to reach out to others in preparation for that glorious event. This preparation begins by committing to 40 days of prayer and devotional study to develop a closer personal relationship with Jesus Christ, and by reaching out to five individuals whom the Lord has put on your heart to pray for every day.

Jesus said, "If two of you agree on earth concerning anything that they ask, it will be done for them by My Father in heaven" (Matt. 18:19). There is great power in united prayer, and there is encouragement and spiritual strength in Christian fellowship.

These devotional studies are divided into five sections, with eight devotionals in each section. Each devotional study is followed by personal reflection and discussion questions, and a prayer focus for the day, which includes a "prayer verse."

If you want to develop a closer relationship with Jesus and reach out to those whom God has put on your heart, who have either once known the truth of God's Word and have slipped away, or have never known the warning message God is giving to prepare the world for Christ's soon return, this book is for you.

Getting Started

As you prepare to embark on this journey, there are a few steps to follow:

1. **Find a prayer partner**. You will be contacting your prayer partner each day to do the following:

    1. Share insights on the reading for the day.

2. Discuss the personal reflection and discussion questions.

3. Pray for each other.

4. Encourage each other to pray for the five people you each have on your list.

5. Remind each other to show the five people on your list that you care.

2. **Pray that God will show you whom you should be praying for.** During the 40 days, you will be praying for five people. Ask God for guidance as you select these individuals.

3. **Choose five people to pray for.** Those on your prayer list may be family members, friends, or coworkers. They may be individuals who have either left the church, or were never members of the church. (If possible, choose individuals living in your area in order to invite them to church sometime during the next 40 days.)

4. **Contact each of the five people you have selected.** You may choose to contact these individuals in person, by phone, by e-mail, or by mail. Following is sample text you can use when contacting the individuals you have selected:

Beginning _____ my church is having a special emphasis on prayer, and is requesting that we choose five individuals to pray for during the next 40 days.

Since you are _____ (examples: my friend, my neighbor, my coworker) it seemed only natural that I would think of praying for you. I would be honored if you would let me know what your specific prayer requests are so that I can know how to pray for you for the next 40 days.

I hope to hear from you soon. I'll keep in touch. Thank you, and God bless!

5. Create a prayer card for each individual to keep you on track. Following is a sample card:

Name:
_____

Phone:
_____

E-mail:
_____

Address:
_____
_____

Prayer Requests:
_____
_____
_____
_____

40 Days of Prayer:
__ __ __ __ __ __ __ __ __ __
__ __ __ __ __ __ __ __ __ __
__ __ __ __ __ __ __ __ __ __
__ __ __ __ __ __ __ __ __ __

Caring Activities:
_____
_____
_____
_____

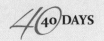

6. **Pray for these individuals every day.** As you pray, claim the Scriptures below on their behalf. These are taken from the *Praying Church Source Book*, pages 128, 129.

1. That God will draw them to Himself (John 6:44)
2. That they seek to know God (Acts 17:27)
3. That they believe the Word of God (1 Thess. 2:13)
4. That Satan be bound from blinding them to the truth and that his influences in their life be "cast down" (2 Cor. 4:4; 10:4, 5)
5. That the Holy Spirit work in them (John 16:8-13)
6. That they turn from sin (Acts 3:19)
7. That they believe in Christ as Savior (John 1:12)
8. That they obey Christ as Lord (Matt. 7:21)
9. That they take root and grow in Christ (Col. 2:6, 7)

7. **Prayerfully consider what activities you can do to show you care.** The following list contains suggestions of things you can do for those on your prayer list to show that you care for them. Add to this list as the Lord leads.

1. Tell them what you appreciate about them.
2. Send them a piece of encouraging literature.
3. Call and pray with them.
4. Invite them to dinner at your home.
5. Invite them to go out to lunch with you.
6. Send them a birthday card.
7. Send them a card expressing encouragement or what God puts in your heart.
8. Take them something you cooked.
9. Invite them to go shopping or to a museum, etc.
10. Send them a get well or sympathy card when needed.
11. Give their child a birthday card and gift when appropriate.
12. Invite them to attend church with you.
13. At the appropriate time ask if they would like to receive Bible studies.

The Power of Prayer

Prayer is essential for one's personal spiritual growth and is the most effective means of reaching others for Christ. Concerning prayer and the Christian's spiritual growth, Ellen White wrote:

"Prayer is the breath of the soul. It is the secret of spiritual power. No other means of grace can be substituted, and the health of the soul be preserved. Prayer brings the heart into immediate contact with the Well-spring of life, and strengthens the sinew and muscle of the religious experience" (*Gospel Workers*, p. 254, 255).

Mrs. White also recognized the necessity of prayer in leading others to Christ:

"Through much prayer you must labor for souls, for this is the only method by which you can reach hearts. It is not your work, but the work of Christ who is by your side, that impresses hearts" (*Evangelism*, p. 342).

As you prayerfully work to bring others closer to Christ and His church, God will bless your efforts. When you pray for, and work for, those on your prayer list, God will not only use you to win others to Christ; He will draw you closer to Himself.

To facilitate the prayer emphasis of this program, there is a "Prayer Activity" section at the end of each day's devotional that offers a suggested prayer focus for the day, and incorporates Bible verses to include in your prayer. (The regular type gives the verse, and the italicized type gives an example of a prayer you can use to pray the verse.)

The Power of the Holy Spirit

After His resurrection, Jesus told His disciples that they were to wait to receive the baptism of the Holy Spirit before they went forth to proclaim the gospel to the world (Luke 24:49; Acts 1:4-8). Even though they had spent the past

three and a half years daily with Christ and had seen and participated in a ministry of miracles, they were not ready to witness for Him. They were to wait to receive the power of the Holy Spirit.

Because the baptism of the Holy Spirit (also called the infilling of the Spirit) is so vital to our personal spiritual growth and our witness to others, these 40 devotional lessons will be based on this important teaching in God's Word.

By choosing to participate in 40 days of study and prayer, you are entering into an amazing and blessed adventure with the Lord. You will experience a deeper relationship with Christ, and you will see the Lord use you to draw others closer to Him in preparation for His soon return. As you fellowship with your prayer partner and the others participating in the program, you will experience a deeper Christian love and unity with your fellow believers. This will play an important role in your personal spiritual growth.

Note: 40 DAYS *is designed also to work along with "Light America Mission," a program of personal spiritual growth through the study of God's Word, prayer, training, and community outreach to share the three angels' messages.*

Information on how to conduct a 40 days program of devotional study and prayer in your church is available at www.40daysdevotional.com. A free downloadable Instruction Manual is located on the Web site.

"If ye then, being evil, know how to give good gifts unto your children: how much more shall your heavenly Father give the Holy Spirit to them that ask him?" (Luke 11:13).

Day 1

The Baptism of the Holy Spirit

Two Works of the Holy Spirit

Scripture testifies that there are many works of the Holy Spirit. One is to lead us to repent, accept Christ, and be baptized in water. This work of the Spirit is for everyone. Another work of the Holy Spirit is to fill the Christian with His presence so he or she can truly live the Christian life and do the works of God. This work of the Spirit is for those who know God. For Jesus said:

"And I will pray the Father, and He will give you another Helper, that He may abide with you forever, even the Spirit of truth, whom the world cannot receive, because it neither sees Him nor knows Him; but you know Him, for He dwells with you and will be in you" (John 14:16, 17).

Jesus indicated that on, and after, the day of Pentecost the baptism of the Holy Spirit became available to every believer when He said that He "will be in you." This wonderful infilling-of-the-Spirit experience is available to you today.

Jesus is our example in all things. He was "born" of the Spirit, led by the Spirit from childhood into manhood, and baptized in water. After the Spirit's infilling He was prepared to go forth in the power of the Spirit to do battle with Satan as never before. Luke 4:1-13 gives the dramatic account of Satan's temptations and Jesus' reliance on the Word of God.

After communing with God in the wilderness and gaining victory over Satan, Jesus was empowered to preach and teach the kingdom of God, carry on a ministry of healing, and cast out devils:

"Then Jesus returned in the power of the Spirit to Galilee, and news of Him went out through all the surrounding region. And He taught in their synagogues, being glorified by all" (verses 14, 15).

Jesus said all who believe on Him would do even greater works than He did:

"Most assuredly, I say to you, he who believes in Me, the works that I do he will do also; and greater works than these he will do, because I go to My Father" (John 14:12).

Before experiencing the Spirit's infilling, God was already with the believer because through the Holy Spirit, God called and led him/her to accept Christ. However, Christians will never experience the fullness of Christ's power unless we allow the Holy Spirit to fill us every day.

Jesus told the disciples to wait for the outpouring of the Spirit on the day of Pentecost before they went forth to preach the gospel:

"And being assembled together with them, He commanded them not to depart from Jerusalem, but to wait for the Promise of the Father, 'which,' He said, 'you have heard from Me; for John truly baptized with water, but you shall be baptized with the Holy Spirit not many days from now'. . . . 'But you shall receive power when the Holy Spirit has come upon you; and you shall be witnesses to Me in Jerusalem, and in all Judea and Samaria, and to the end of the earth'" (Acts 1:4-8).

The baptism of the Holy Spirit is available to every Christian today. God has promised to give the Spirit in fullness to us if we ask in faith (Luke 11:13).

Some may ask, "How can I make sure that I am prepared to receive the Holy Spirit?" Your response to the following questions will help you answer this. Have you received Christ as your Savior? Have you decided to commit your life daily to Jesus?

If you have accepted Christ and desire to follow Him in every aspect of your life, and if it is your desire to receive the Holy Spirit, I invite you to pray the following prayer:

"Father, I thank You for leading me to accept Jesus Christ as my Savior, and I ask You to forgive me for all my sins. I desire to commit my life 100 percent to Jesus. I thank You for the promise to fill me with Your Spirit and claim the promise of the baptism of the Holy Spirit in my life right now. I pray that You will so infill me with the presence of Jesus that His character will be fully manifested through me. I claim Your promise to empower me by Your Spirit to serve You as You lead me into ministry for Jesus. In Jesus' name, amen."

Personal Reflection and Discussion

1. What does this lesson teach about the work of the Holy Spirit?

_____

_____

2. List two ways we can prepare to receive the Holy Spirit.

_____

_____

3. List two benefits of receiving the baptism of the Holy Spirit.

_____

_____

4. Do you desire to have a deeper experience of the Holy Spirit in your life and service for the Lord? Tell your prayer partner.

_____

Prayer Activity

- Call your prayer partner and discuss this devotional with him/her.
- Pray with your prayer partner:
    1. for God to fill each of you with His Holy Spirit.
    2. for God to open your understanding as you study your daily devotional.
    3. for God to bless you and your prayer partner's fellowship.
    4. for the individuals on your prayer list.

INCLUDE THE FOLLOWING BIBLE VERSE IN YOUR PRAYER: "I will instruct you and teach you in the way you should go; I will guide you with My eye" (Ps. 32:8).

Guide and teach us, Lord, that we will constantly be under Your direction in our lives and church.

Day 2

Receiving the Holy Spirit After Pentecost

Jesus promised to baptize His followers with the Holy Spirit so that they would be empowered to take the gospel to the world. This promise was fulfilled on the day of Pentecost:

"When the Day of Pentecost had fully come, they were all with one accord in one place. And suddenly there came a sound from heaven, as of a rushing mighty wind, and it filled the whole house where they were sitting. Then there appeared to them divided tongues, as of fire, and one sat upon each of them. And they were all filled with the Holy Spirit and began to speak with other tongues, as the Spirit gave them utterance" (Acts 2:1-4).

The baptism of the Holy Spirit was not only for the disciples at Pentecost; this experience was, and is, for all Christians since that time.

Not every believer was present at Pentecost. A practical question might be, How did Christians receive the baptism of the Spirit after Pentecost? The answer is found in the book of Acts. On at least two occasions the Spirit fell on a group while Peter spoke to them. Let's look at one occasion in Acts 10:44-47:

"While Peter was still speaking these words, the Holy Spirit fell upon all those who heard the word. And those of the circumcision who believed were astonished, as many as came with Peter, because the gift of the Holy Spirit had been poured out on the Gentiles also. For they heard them speak with tongues and magnify God. Then Peter answered, "'Can anyone forbid water, that these should not be baptized who have received the Holy Spirit just as we have?'"

It appears that God also led the church to receive the baptism of the Spirit by the laying on of hands. "But when they believed Philip preaching the things concerning the kingdom of God, and the name of Jesus Christ, they were baptized, both men and women. Then Simon himself believed also: and when he was baptized, he continued with Philip, and wondered, beholding the miracles and signs which were done. Now when the apostles which were at Jerusalem heard that Samaria had received the word of God, they sent unto them Peter and John: who, when they were come down, prayed for them, that they might receive the Holy Ghost: (For as yet he was fallen upon none of them: only they were baptized in the name of the Lord Jesus.) Then laid they their hands on them, and they received the Holy Ghost" (Acts 8:12-17).

We find a similar example of prayer with laying on of hands when Paul met with disciples in Ephesus (Acts 19:1-6).

The one performing this prayer with laying on of hands should be a believer who has received the baptism of the Holy Spirit himself/herself. It should also be pointed out that the laying on of hands is not necessary to receive the baptism of the Holy Spirit. It is a wonderful experience to seek the Spirit's infilling in this manner; however, it is not necessary. Receiving the baptism of the Spirit is simply a matter of claiming by faith God's promise of the Spirit:

"That the blessing of Abraham might come upon the Gentiles through Jesus Christ, that we might receive the promise of the Spirit through faith" (Gal. 3:14).

The promised Spirit is received through faith at our baptism but we need to seek the infilling of the Holy Spirit daily in order to witness effectively to others. Ellen White wrote:

"What we need is the baptism of the Holy Spirit. Without this, we are no more fitted to go forth to the world than were the disciples after the crucifixion of their Lord" (*Review and Herald,* Feb. 18, 1890).

Concerning our personal spiritual growth and the Spirit's infilling, she wrote:

> *Jesus promised to baptize His followers with the Holy Spirit so they would be empowered to take the gospel to the world.*

"Impress upon all the necessity of the baptism of the Holy Spirit, the sanctification of the members of the church, so that they will be living, growing, fruit-bearing trees of the Lord's planting" (*Testimonies for the Church*, vol. 6, p. 86).

When one reads Ellen White's statements it is clear that she saw its importance and urged every believer to seek the fullness of the Spirit in his/her life.

15

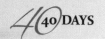
Personal Reflection and Discussion

1. Why did Jesus tell the disciples to wait for the baptism of the Holy Spirit?

_____

_____

2. What were the conditions under which the disciples received the baptism of the Holy Spirit?

_____

_____

3. What did Ellen White say about the importance of receiving the baptism of the Holy Spirit?

_____

_____

4. Is prayer with laying on of hands necessary to receive the baptism of the Holy Spirit? Explain your answer.

_____

_____

Prayer Activity

- Call your prayer partner and discuss this devotional with him/her.
- Pray with your prayer partner:
    1. for God to fill each of you with His Holy Spirit.
    2. for God to minister through you in the power of the Spirit.
    3. for the individuals on your prayer list.

INCLUDE THE FOLLOWING BIBLE VERSE IN YOUR PRAYER: "And we are His witnesses to these things, and so also is the Holy Spirit whom God has given to those who obey Him" (Acts 5:32).

Benefits of Receiving the Holy Spirit

What happens when we ask God for the baptism of the Holy Spirit? A few examples of the changes the infilling of the Spirit will bring to the life of the receiver are: (1) a stronger desire to study God's Word, (2) a more earnest prayer life, (3) a deeper repentance for our sins, and (4) changes in lifestyles and activities.

The infilling of the Spirit is necessary for the believer to walk victoriously in Christ. According to the Bible, one does not "know" Christ in the fullest biblical sense without the baptism of the Holy Spirit. This is illustrated in the parable of the ten virgins (Matt. 25:1-13), in which Christ told the foolish virgins, who were without the oil of the Holy Spirit, "I do not know you" (verse 12).

Here, as well as in other Scriptures, Christ speaks of not "knowing" someone. For example, Jesus said:

"Not everyone who says to Me, 'Lord, Lord,' shall enter the kingdom of heaven, but he who does the will of My Father in heaven. Many will say to Me in that day, 'Lord, Lord, have we not prophesied in Your name, cast out demons in Your name, and done many wonders in Your name?' And then I will declare to them, 'I never knew you; depart from Me, you who practice lawlessness!'" (Matt. 7:21-23).

Simply knowing the teachings of the Bible, or engaging in active ministry for Jesus, is not a substitute for knowing Him intimately through the baptism of the Holy Spirit.

Water baptism is similar to the wedding service, while Spirit baptism is symbolized by the consummation of the marriage when the bride "knows" her bridegroom. Satan will resist this work fiercely; for he is aware that the Spirit's infilling will break his power in the believer's life.

Understanding and experiencing the infilling of the Holy Spirit is second in importance only to understanding and accepting Christ as our Savior. Another very important point is that we must renew this infilling every day. It is not a "once and forever" experience. Paul tells us that "the inward man is being renewed day by day" (2 Cor. 4:16). We need the renewing of the Spirit every day of our lives. Paul's command to "be filled with the Spirit" (Eph. 5:18) is a continuous action verb in the Greek, meaning we are to keep on being filled with the Spirit daily.

Christ is our example in all things. Ellen White wrote:

"Daily He received a fresh baptism of the Holy Spirit. In the early hours of the new day the Lord awakened Him from His slumbers, and His soul and His lips were anointed with grace, that He might impart to others" (*Christ's Object Lessons,* p. 139).

If Christ worked so closely with the Holy Spirit while He was on earth, Christians surely need to pray for the daily presence of the Holy Spirit in their lives.

Our growth into the fullness of Christ by the Spirit is a process:

"But we all, with unveiled face, beholding as in a mirror the glory of the Lord, are being transformed into the same image from glory to glory, just as by the Spirit of the Lord" (2 Cor. 3:18).

Spiritual growth is a process into which we must enter anew every day. Ellen White described the development of character the recipient of the Spirit's infilling receives when she wrote:

> *Understanding and experiencing the infilling of the Holy Spirit is second in importance only to understanding and accepting Christ as our Savior.*

"When the Spirit of God takes possession of the heart, it transforms the life. Sinful thoughts are put away, evil deeds are renounced; love, humility, and peace take the place of anger, envy, and strife. Joy takes the place of sadness, and the countenance reflects the light of heaven" (*The Desire of Ages,* p. 173).

What a wonderful blessing our Lord has provided for each of us through the baptism of the Holy Spirit!

Personal Reflection and Discussion

1. List four benefits of receiving the baptism of the Holy Spirit.

_____

_____

2. How often is the Christian to ask for the infilling of the Holy Spirit?

_____

_____

3. What does Ellen White say will happen in our lives when we receive the baptism of the Holy Spirit?

_____

_____

Prayer Activity

- Call your prayer partner and discuss this devotional with him/her.
- Pray with your prayer partner:
    1. for God to continue to fill each of you with His Holy Spirit.
    2. for Christ to manifest the changes in your life necessary for you to reflect Him.
    3. for the individuals on your prayer list.

INCLUDE THE FOLLOWING BIBLE VERSE IN YOUR PRAYER:
"Behold, the eye of the Lord is on those who fear Him, on those who hope in His mercy, to deliver their soul from death, and to keep them alive in famine. Our soul waits for the Lord; He is our help and our shield. For our heart shall rejoice in Him, because we have trusted in His holy name. Let Your mercy, O Lord, be upon us, just as we hope in You" (Ps. 33:18-22).

Turn our hope to You, Lord, and not to earthly things. Deliver us from our spiritually dead condition. Bring us back to spiritual life, from our condition of spiritual famine. Be our help and shield—cause us to rejoice in You.

Day 4

Christ in You

When believers receive the baptism of the Holy Spirit, they are actually receiving Christ more fully into their life. Jesus foretold this when He promised His disciples another Comforter that the Father would send to dwell with them and "be in" them:

"And I will pray the Father, and He will give you another Helper, that He may abide with you forever, even the Spirit of truth, whom the world cannot receive, because it neither sees Him nor knows Him; but you know Him, for He dwells with you and will be in you" (John 14:16, 17).

This Comforter is the Holy Spirit. Then Jesus said:

"I will not leave you orphans; I will come to you" (verse 18).

Hence, through the Holy Spirit Jesus comes to "dwell with" and "be in" His people. It is through the Spirit's infilling that Jesus most fully lives within His disciples:

"Now he who keeps His commandments abides in Him, and He in him. And by this we know that He abides in us, by the Spirit whom He has given us" (1 John 3:24).

John tells us that when Jesus comes, His true followers "shall be like Him:"

"Beloved, now we are children of God; and it has not yet been revealed what we shall be, but we know that when He is revealed, we shall be like Him, for we shall see Him as He is" (verse 2).

How much like Jesus are we to become? The Greek word translated "like" means "just like" Him. How will this happen? The daily infilling of the Holy Spirit now prepares us to be just like Him when He comes.

"I have been crucified with Christ; it is no longer I who live, but Christ lives in me; and the life which I now live in the flesh I live by faith in the Son of God, who loved me and gave Himself for me" (Gal. 2:20).

Through the infilling of the Holy Spirit, Christ will come and live in each of us. Because of Christ's indwelling presence the Spirit-filled believer will have the mind of Christ—the love of righteousness and sanctification, and hatred of sin:

"For 'who has known the mind of the Lord that he may instruct Him?' But we have the mind of Christ" (1 Cor. 2:16).

The same passion for souls that Christ has will be in them, and they will seek to obey the Father. Paul tells us the wisdom (righteousness) and holiness of Christ is theirs:

Every virtue and quality of Christ dwells in the Spirit-filled believer because Christ dwells in them.

"That no flesh should glory in His presence. But of Him you are in Christ Jesus, who became for us wisdom from God—and righteousness and sanctification and redemption—that, as it is written, 'He who glories, let him glory in the Lord'" (1 Cor. 1:29-31).

Every virtue and quality of Christ dwells in the Spirit-filled believer because Christ dwells in them. Paul indicated this when he wrote, "Christ is [being] formed in you" (Gal. 4:19). They will become more and more like Christ every day as they are changed into His image "from glory to glory, just as by the Spirit of the Lord" (2 Cor. 3:18).

As the Spirit takes a fuller possession of the believer's life, they will become like Jesus in every way (1 John 3:2) and the fruit of the Spirit will be modeled (Gal. 5:22, 23).

This happens when the believer receives the baptism of the Holy Spirit and continues to walk in the Spirit. The believer becomes as Christ to the world. We become Christ's mouth, hands, and feet, doing the works He did—preaching, teaching, healing, casting out devils.

Christ's presence dwelling in the believer through the baptism of the Holy Spirit is the Christian's only hope of His glory being revealed in, and through, them:

"To them God willed to make known what are the riches of the glory of this mystery among the Gentiles: which is Christ in you, the hope of glory" (Col. 1:27).

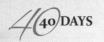

Personal Reflection and Discussion

1. When believers receive the baptism of the Holy Spirit, who else do they receive?

_____

_____

2. What will the Christian be like when Christ dwells in him/her through the Holy Spirit?

_____

_____

_____

Prayer Activity

- Call your prayer partner and discuss this devotional with him/her.
- Pray with your prayer partner:
    1. for God to continue to baptize each of you with His Holy Spirit.
    2. for Christ to live in you fully, and manifest His character and works in you.
    3. for the individuals on your prayer list.
    4. for God to continue to guide you with His Holy Spirit.

INCLUDE THE FOLLOWING BIBLE VERSE IN YOUR PRAYER: "And what agreement has the temple of God with idols? For you are the temple of the living God. As God has said: 'I will dwell in them and walk among them. I will be their God, and they shall be My people'" (2 Cor. 6:16).

Hear us and deliver us from the things that hinder us from growing fully in Christ, individually, and as a congregation. We need You and want You in our lives.

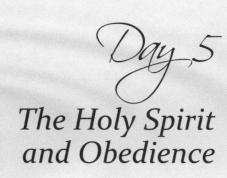

Day 5

The Holy Spirit and Obedience

One of the purposes of the Holy Spirit is to help us to reflect Jesus more fully in our lives. God's goal is that Christ be seen in us, that we be a living letter revealing the character of Christ. Another purpose of the Spirit's infilling is to receive power for witnessing.

In today's devotional we will focus on reflecting Jesus' character.

The professed Christian can participate in two kinds of obedience. First is what I call external obedience. This could lead to legalism if the believer obeys the law of God because they are seeking the reward of salvation on this basis alone. God wants us to trust Him and obey Him from the heart. The second form of obedience is internal obedience, and occurs because of a deep, inner desire within the believer to obey God. External obedience without heart obedience is unacceptable to God:

"For You do not desire sacrifice, or else I would give it; You do not delight in burnt offering. The sacrifices of God are a broken spirit, a broken and a contrite heart—these, O God, You will not despise" (Ps. 51:16, 17).

God's goal is that Christ be seen in us, that we be a living letter revealing the character of Christ.

"These people draw near to Me with their mouth, and honor Me with their lips, but their heart is far from Me" (Matt. 15:8).

I came across an illustration many years ago that clarifies the difference between external and internal obedience. Let's say my father died, and I'm not sure if I should mourn his death, or not, so I go to a friend and ask his advice. We discuss whether or not I should mourn. My friend finally says, "After all, he was your father, and you are his son. So I think you should

mourn his death." On his advice I begin mourning my father's death. I think it becomes obvious that my mourning in this case would not be genuine mourning from the heart. Rather, it would be external mourning because it was my obligation, as my father's son, to mourn his death. True mourning would come spontaneously from the heart. I couldn't help mourning if it were genuine mourning. The same is true of obedience to God. When one is in right relationship with God through the infilling of the Spirit, obedience springs naturally and spontaneously from the heart without even thinking about it. Temptations to disobey will come; however, they will be much weakened in influence by the strong desire God has placed in the heart to obey.

Through the baptism, or infilling of the Holy Spirit, God's law is written in our hearts, and we obey from the heart. This does not fully happen when we accept Christ and are baptized by water. Paul states that we must continually be "filled with the Spirit," which is necessary for God's law to continue to be written on our heart:

"And do not be drunk with wine, in which is dissipation; but be filled with the Spirit" (Eph. 5:18).

Ellen White described this "internal" obedience, which springs from daily experiencing the baptism of the Holy Spirit, when she wrote:

"All true obedience comes from the heart. It was heart work with Christ. And if we consent, He will so identify Himself with our thoughts and aims, so blend our hearts and minds into conformity to His will, that when obeying Him we shall be but carrying out our own impulses. The will, refined and sanctified, will find its highest delight in doing His service. When we know God, as it is our privilege to know Him, our life will be a life of continual obedience. Through an appreciation of the character of Christ, through communion with God, sin will become hateful to us" (*The Desire of Ages,* p. 668).

Lord, remove from me my sinful heart and prideful spirit. In mercy bring me close to You, and restore the fullness of Your Spirit to me. Bring me to experience the full joy of Your salvation, and give me Your strength.

Personal Reflection and Discussion

1. From this lesson what are two purposes of receiving the Holy Spirit?

_____

_____

2. What are two types of obedience that professed Christians can participate in?

_____

_____

3. What kind of obedience does God desire?

_____

_____

4. How does Ellen White describe obedience from the heart?

_____

_____

Prayer Activity

- Continue your efforts to contact all of the individuals on your prayer list to tell them you are praying for them, and ask them what they want you to pray for on their behalf.
- Call your prayer partner and discuss this devotional with him/her.
- Pray with your prayer partner:
    1. for God to continue to fill each of you with His Holy Spirit.
    2. for God to write His law on your heart.
    3. for the individuals on your prayer list.
    4. for God to continue to fill each of you with His Holy Spirit.

INCLUDE THE FOLLOWING BIBLE VERSE IN YOUR PRAYER:
"Create in me a clean heart, O God, and renew a steadfast spirit within me. Do not cast me away from Your presence, and do not take Your Holy Spirit from me. Restore to me the joy of Your salvation, and uphold me with Your generous Spirit" (Ps. 51:10-12).

Day 6

Grieving the Holy Spirit

There are things we can do that will grieve the Spirit. If we do not daily seek Him and cooperate in following where He leads us, our Christian experience will weaken.

God doesn't force. When we receive the baptism of the Spirit, He will have a greater impact in our life. We will feel His prompting more strongly. He will be daily putting the desire in our heart to obey God. He will call us to study God's Word and to pray more. The Spirit will cause us to begin loving righteousness and hating sin. However, we are always free to disregard His prompting. When we do this we begin the process of "grieving," or "quenching," the Spirit. Paul gives practical advice in many portions of Scripture on how to avoid doing this. These practical counsels to the believer on living the Christian life are intended to help us maintain the fullness of the Spirit in our lives. Two examples of such counsel are found in the following Bible verses:

"And that you put on the new man which was created according to God, in righteousness and true holiness. Therefore, putting away lying, each one speak truth with his neighbor, for we are members of one another. 'Be angry, and do not sin': do not let the sun go down on your wrath, nor give place to the devil. Let him who stole steal no longer, but rather let him labor, working with his hands what is good, that he may have something to give him who has need. Let no corrupt communication proceed out of your mouth, but what is good for necessary edification, that it may impart grace to the hearers. And do not grieve the Holy Spirit of God, by whom you were sealed for the day of redemption. Let all bitterness, wrath, anger, clamor, and evil speaking be put away from you, with all malice. And be kind to one another, tenderhearted, forgiving one another, even as God in Christ forgave you" (Eph. 4:24-32).

"Now we exhort you, brethren, warn those who are unruly, comfort the fainthearted, uphold the weak, be patient with all. See that no one renders evil for evil to anyone, but always pursue what is good both for yourselves and for all. Rejoice always, pray without ceasing, in everything give thanks; for this is the will of God in Christ Jesus for you. Do not quench the Spirit" (1 Thess. 5:14-19).

Paul knew that the Spirit of God dwelling in believers would be prompting them to do the things listed in these verses. If we refuse to yield to His prompting, though, we will be in danger of grieving and quenching the Spirit.

If you find that you have grieved the Spirit, don't become discouraged! Ask God to forgive you, and He will (1 John 1:9). Then ask God in faith to fill you anew with His Spirit, and He will do that, too (Luke 11:13).

David knew God's mercy. He had committed the sins of adultery and murder. He had walked away from the prompting of God's Spirit in his life when he committed these terrible acts. Yet when he was convicted of his sin by the Spirit, he turned to God in prayer. Note especially these words:

When we find that we've been slipping away from God we must not let another moment go by without confessing our sin.

"Hide Your face from my sins, and blot out all my iniquities. Create in me a clean heart, O God, and renew a steadfast spirit within me. Do not cast me away from Your presence, and do not take Your Holy Spirit from me. Restore to me the joy of Your salvation, and uphold me with Your generous Spirit" (Ps. 51:9-12).

When we find that we've been slipping away from God we must not let another moment go by without confessing our sin, accepting God's forgiveness, and claiming the promise of the renewing of the Spirit in our lives just as David did. Then we will be strengthened once again in the "inner" man to be victorious over Satan:

"That He would grant you, according to the riches of His glory, to be strengthened with might through His Spirit in the inner man, that Christ may dwell in your hearts through faith; that you, being rooted and grounded in love, may be able to comprehend with all the saints what is the width and length and depth and height—to know the love of Christ

which passes knowledge; that you may be filled with all the fullness of God" (Eph. 3:16-19).

We serve a wonderful God. When we have failed Him, let us remember:

"The Lord is merciful and gracious, slow to anger, and abounding in mercy. He will not always strive with us, nor will He keep His anger forever. He has not dealt with us according to our sins, nor punished us according to our iniquities. For as the heavens are high above the earth, so great is His mercy toward those who fear Him; as far as the east is from the west, so far has He removed our transgressions from us. As a father pities his children, so the Lord pities those who fear Him" (Ps. 103:8-13).

Make our hearts fully committed to You. Show Yourself strong on our behalf to bring about the needed changes in us that we will experience the revival and reformation we need. Forgive us when we have fallen short of Your plan.

Personal Reflection and Discussion

1. List some behaviors and attitudes the Holy Spirit seeks to bring into the Christian's life.

_____

_____

2. How does a Christian grieve the Holy Spirit?

_____

_____

3. If we have grieved the Holy Spirit, what should we do?

_____

_____

4. What is God's attitude toward His children?

_____

_____

Prayer Activity

- Call your prayer partner and discuss this devotional with him/her.
- Pray with your prayer partner:
    1. for God to continue to baptize each of you with His Holy Spirit.
    2. for God to forgive you if you have grieved the Holy Spirit in any way.
    3. for God to give you the desire to yield to the Spirit's promptings in your life.
    4. for the individuals on your prayer list.
    5. that we continue to seek the Holy Spirit.

INCLUDE THE FOLLOWING BIBLE VERSE IN YOUR PRAYER:
"For the eyes of the Lord run to and fro throughout the whole earth, to show Himself strong on behalf of those whose heart is loyal [fully committed (NIV)] to Him" (2 Chron. 16:9).

Day 7

The Latter Rain

It is vital that we daily walk in the Holy Spirit in order to grow spiritually and be prepared to receive the latter rain of the Spirit, which prepares God's people for the final crisis and Christ's return. However, many don't realize this and feel that they must wait for the latter rain of the Spirit if they are finally to have the victory over their besetting sins and spiritual immaturity. Such a view will end in disaster for the one who holds it. Ellen White warned:

"I saw that many were neglecting the preparation so needful and were looking to the time of 'refreshing' and the 'latter rain' to fit them to stand in the day of the Lord and to live in His sight. Oh, how many I saw in the time of trouble without a shelter! They had neglected the needful preparation, therefore they could not receive the refreshing that all must have to fit them to live in the sight of a holy God" (*Early Writings,* p. 71).

We must have victory over all temptation and sin in our life if we are to benefit from the latter rain outpouring of the Spirit. It is a deception of Satan if we believe we do not have to take seriously the sin problem in our lives:

"Repent therefore and be converted, that your sins may be blotted out, so that times of refreshing may come from the presence of the Lord" (Acts 3:19).

"Knowing this, that our old man was crucified with Him, that the body of sin might be done away with, that we should no longer be slaves of sin. . . . Likewise you also, reckon yourselves to be dead indeed to sin, but alive to God in Christ Jesus our Lord. Therefore do not let sin reign in your mortal body, that you should obey it in its lusts. And do not present your members as instruments of unrighteousness to sin, but present yourselves to God as being alive from the dead, and your members as instruments of righteousness to God. For sin shall not have dominion over you, for you are not under law but under grace" (Rom. 6:6, 11-14).

Ellen White confirmed this with these words:

"I saw that none could share the 'refreshing' [latter rain] unless they obtained the victory over every besetment, over pride, selfishness, love of the world, and over every wrong word and action" (Ibid.).

This may sound impossible to you right now. However, the key to victory over temptation is in learning how to let Jesus live out His life of victory in, and through, us. That wonderful biblical truth will be presented later in this devotional series.

That the Holy Spirit would be poured out in the last days was clearly taught by Peter quoting the prophet Joel in the book of Acts. What happened at Pentecost, according to Peter was a direct fulfillment of that prophecy. Peter pointed this out when he said to the crowd on that day:

"But this is what was spoken by the prophet Joel: 'And it shall come to pass in the last days, says God, that I will pour out of My Spirit on all flesh; your sons and your daughters shall prophesy, your young men shall see visions, your old men shall dream dreams.

> *The key to victory over temptation is in learning how to let Jesus live out His life of victory in, and through, us.*

And on My menservants and on My maidservants I will pour out My Spirit in those days; and they shall prophesy" (Acts 2:16-18).

Ellen White gave the following description of a latter rain blessing that will come before the end of time to prepare God's children for Jesus' Second Coming:

"The latter rain, ripening earth's harvest, represents the spiritual grace that prepares the church for the coming of the Son of man. But unless the former rain has fallen, there will be no life; the green blade will not spring up. Unless the early showers have done their work, the latter rain can bring no seed to perfection" (*The Faith I Live By,* p. 333).

Daily spiritual growth in the grace of Christ and the work of the Holy Spirit is necessary for us to be able even to recognize the latter rain of the Spirit when it is falling. Ellen White pointed this out when she wrote:

"Unless we are daily advancing in the exemplification of the active

Christian virtues, we shall not recognize the manifestations of the Holy Spirit in the latter rain. It may be falling on hearts all around us, but we shall not discern or receive it" (*Testimonies to Ministers and Gospel Workers,* p. 507).

If you have not received the Holy Spirit's infilling, don't delay another day. His reception should be first and foremost in our lives, for this Gift will bring all other gifts to us. The Spirit's infilling will bring us into a closer relationship with Jesus and change our lethargy to excitement, our weakness to strength, and our witness will become greater than what we have ever experienced before:

"I have been crucified with Christ; it is no longer I who live, but Christ lives in me; and the life which I now live in the flesh I live by faith in the Son of God, who loved me and gave Himself for me" (Gal. 2:20).

Deliver us from our state of spiritual lethargy and protect us from Satan's attacks. Prepare us for the latter rain.

Personal Reflection and Discussion

1. What metaphor is used to describe the outpouring of the Holy Spirit in the Bible?

_____

_____

2. How necessary is it for the Christian to receive the baptism of the Spirit in order to benefit from the latter rain of the Spirit? Why is it necessary for the Christian to have already received the Holy Spirit prior to the latter rain?

_____

_____

3. What changes must happen in the Christian's life after the baptism of the Holy Spirit to be ready for the latter rain?

_____

_____

4. Why is it not wise to wait for the latter rain before we take the sin problem in our life seriously?

_____

_____

Prayer Activity

- Call your prayer partner and discuss this devotional with him/her.
- Pray with your prayer partner:
  1. for God to continue to strengthen each of you with His Holy Spirit.
  2. for God to prepare you to receive the latter rain of the Spirit.
  3. for the individuals on your prayer list.

INCLUDE THE FOLLOWING BIBLE VERSE IN YOUR PRAYER:
"The angel of the Lord encamps all around those who fear Him, and delivers them" (Ps. 34:7).

Day 8

The Holy Spirit and Christ's Return

The good news for today is that Jesus is coming soon! I don't say this only because of terrorist attacks, world conflicts, epidemic outbreaks, or natural disasters—all these certainly indicate Christ's return is soon. However, there is something else that convicts me even more that Christ's coming is imminent. It is His moving among us to understand and to daily receive the Holy Spirit.

The last verses of Revelation 6 describe Jesus' coming and ask the question who shall be able to stand? meaning, who will be able to survive the event? The answer is found in Revelation 7:1-3:

"After these things I saw four angels standing at the four corners of the earth, holding the four winds of the earth, that the wind should not blow on the earth, on the sea, or on any tree. Then I saw another angel ascending from the east, having the seal of the living God. And he cried with a loud voice to the four angels to whom it was granted to harm the earth and the sea, saying, 'Do not harm the earth, the sea, or the trees till we have sealed the servants of our God on their foreheads.'"

Only those who have the seal of God will be able to survive the second coming of Christ. In fact, God is holding back many destructive forces in this earth until God's people are sealed. An important question, then, is how are we sealed? The Bible says we are sealed by the Holy Spirit:

"And do not grieve the Holy Spirit of God, by whom you were sealed for the day of redemption" (Eph. 4:30).

That is what the baptism of the Holy Sprit is all about. It is as we daily recommit our lives to Christ and continue to walk in the Holy Spirit that we are sealed and prepared for Christ's second coming.

God is not waiting for more terrorist attacks, disease outbreaks, or natural disasters. Ellen White tells us what Christ is waiting for:

"Christ is waiting with longing desire for the manifestation of Himself in His church. When the character of Christ shall be perfectly reproduced in His people, then He will come to claim them as His own" (*Christ's Object Lessons,* p. 69).

Only by the baptism of the Holy Spirit can this happen in our lives. And only by the baptism of the Holy Spirit can we be ready when the angels let go the winds of destruction. Ellen White writes:

"Nothing but the baptism of the Holy Spirit can bring up the church to its right position, and prepare the people of God for the fast approaching conflict" (*Manuscript Releases,* vol. 2, p. 30).

We have a danger, as Seventh-day Adventists. We think we are secure and will be ready for Christ's return because we know about the Sabbath, the state of the dead, the mark of the beast, and the manner of Christ's second coming. This is a deadly error. These teachings are important; however, this knowledge alone will not save us. Remember, it was tithe-paying, Sabbathkeeping health reformers who crucified Jesus. No; it is not what we know; it is whom we know that will enable us to be saved (John 17:3). We must have an intimate relationship with Jesus Christ if we are to be ready for His return.

Today God is calling His people to receive the baptism of the Holy Spirit in preparation for becoming just like Jesus, in order to receive the latter rain of the Spirit, and to be ready for Christ's return:

"Beloved, now we are children of God; and it has not yet been revealed what we shall be, but we know that when He is revealed, we shall be like Him, for we shall see Him as He is" (1 John 3:2).

However, the church has a problem today. God tells us that we are in a Laodicean condition and, if we don't change, we will not be ready for Christ's return. God also gives us the solution: let Jesus into our lives more fully:

"Behold, I stand at the door and knock. If anyone hears My voice and opens the door, I will come in to him and dine with him, and he with Me" (Rev. 3:20).

How do we let Jesus in and have the intimate relationship with Him that we must have? Ellen White tells us:

"We must have a living connection with God. We must be clothed with power from on high by the baptism of the Holy Spirit that we may reach a higher standard; for there is help for us in no other way" (*Review and Herald,* April 5, 1892).

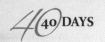

Personal Reflection and Discussion

1. Why are the angels holding back the winds of destruction on this earth?

_____

_____

2. Is knowing the doctrines of the Bible all we need in order to be saved? Why, or why not?

_____

_____

3. According to the Bible, how are we sealed?

_____

_____

4. What does the baptism of the Holy Spirit do for our relationship with Christ?

_____

_____

5. What will prepare us for the final crisis?

_____

_____

Prayer Activity

- Call your prayer partner and discuss this devotional with him/her.
- Pray with your prayer partner:
    1. for God to continue to anoint each of you with His Holy Spirit.
    2. for God to prepare you for earth's final crisis and Christ's return.
    3. for the individuals on your prayer list.

INCLUDE THE FOLLOWING BIBLE VERSE IN YOUR PRAYER:
"The Lord is near to those who have a broken heart, and saves such as have a contrite spirit" (Ps. 34:18).

Day 9

A Spirit-given Desire to Pray

When we receive the baptism of the Holy Spirit, a deep, inner desire will begin to develop within us to be more in prayer to our heavenly Father:

"And I will pour on the house of David and on the inhabitants of Jerusalem the Spirit of grace and supplication" (Zech. 12:10).

We can either yield to this God-given desire, or ignore it. However, if we want to experience the deep things of God and the fullness of Christ in our lives, we must yield to this desire to pray. If we want to see His delivering power manifested in our lives over everything Satan tries to bring on us and to see the power of God manifested through us in blessing others with His deliverance, we must spend much time with God in prayer.

Christians have known the importance of prayer for years. Many times we have made efforts to take time in prayer, but those special seasons of prayer were motivated by some crisis and didn't continue for very long.

Our problem is that we've become very self-sufficient in meeting our own needs and the needs of the church. We have learned to rely on our own efforts to do the work of God. We have been involved in much planning and many programs. We have learned to depend on the "flesh" to do God's work. In

> *A blessing beyond our greatest expectations awaits us when we are baptized and enter into the prayer relationship He desires for us.*

mercy He has blessed our feeble efforts. However, a blessing beyond our greatest expectations awaits us when we are baptized and enter into the prayer relationship He desires for us. Only then will our plans be God's plans, and our activities be God's activities.

Jesus had this kind of meaningful, deep, and powerful relationship with His Father. In fact, this relationship was so close and intimate that Jesus said:

"I and My Father are one" (John 10:30).

Everything Jesus did was under the direction of His Father. His words, His actions were all done under the direction and power of the Father. Jesus emphasized this when He said:

"Do you not believe that I am in the Father, and the Father in Me? The words that I speak to you I do not speak on My own authority; but the Father who dwells in Me does the works" (John 14:10).

How did Jesus obtain such a close oneness with His Father? It was through daily communion with the Father.

From this special communion with His Father, Christ came forth prepared to do the work He came to earth to do. He was empowered to be victorious over Satan and to defeat him:

"Then Jesus returned in the power of the Spirit to Galilee, and news of Him went out through all the surrounding region" (verse 14).

The 40 days of prayer you have chosen to participate in is designed to do the same for you. During these 40 days you will experience empowerment to be victorious over Satan and to be a witness for Christ to minister through you to others.

Lead us into humility. Put in our hearts a desire to be a praying people and to turn from our wicked ways. Hear our prayer, forgive us, and heal us of our backsliding.

Personal Reflection and Discussion

1. In general what do Christians tend to depend on more than prayer? Is this good or bad?

_____

_____

2. What kind of prayer life did Jesus have? How did Jesus describe His relationship with His Father?

_____

_____

3. What kind of prayer life do you think Jesus wants you to have? How will the Holy Spirit affect our prayer life?

_____

_____

Prayer Activity

- Call your prayer partner and discuss this devotional with him/her.
- Pray with your prayer partner:
    1. for God to continue to minister to each of you with His Holy Spirit.
    2. for God to give you a greater desire to pray.
    3. for the individuals on your prayer list.

INCLUDE THE FOLLOWING BIBLE VERSE IN YOUR PRAYER:
"If My people who are called by My name will humble themselves, and pray and seek My face, and turn from their wicked ways, then I will hear from heaven, and will forgive their sin and heal their land" (2 Chron. 7:14).

Day 10

Jesus' and the Disciples' Example of Prayer

Time and again, we see Christ in prayer during His ministry on earth. After teaching great multitudes and healing them of their infirmities, we are told:

"So He Himself often withdrew into the wilderness and prayed" (Luke 5:16).

Luke reports that before calling the 12 disciples:

"Now it came to pass in those days that He went out to the mountain to pray, and continued all night in prayer to God. And when it was day, He called His disciples to Him; and from them He chose twelve whom He also named apostles" (Luke 6:12, 13).

On the Mount of Transfiguration Jesus prayed (Luke 9:29). He was drawn by the Spirit to spend time with His heavenly Father in prayer. He responded to the deep, inner need for prayer that He felt. He knew it was only through such times of prayer that He would be one with the Father and be empowered to do the work He came to do.

Jesus gained His victories over Satan's works through times in prayer with the Father. When we read of Christ confronting Satan in the lives of men and women and nature in the forms of devil possession, disease, death, storm, etc., we do not see Christ at that moment in deep prayer with His Father, praying for the power to deliver. He had already received that power from the Father during the times of intimate prayer seasons. When confronted with Satan and his works, Jesus simply spoke the word in the power and authority of the Father, and Satan's power was broken. Christ's word cast out devils, healed the sick, raised the dead, and quelled the storm.

The lesson is clear. Christ maintained His oneness with the Father and received His power over the enemy during His seasons of prayer with the Father. He then came away from these prayer times taking the Father with Him. He was conscious of the Father's presence moment by moment and day by day. Christ maintained this conscious and very real oneness with the Father throughout His life. Whenever He was confronted with Satan, He was prepared to meet the challenge and gain the victory because of His prayer life.

The example of Christ's prayer life was not lost on the disciples. Prayer was a central part of their ministry. When the growth of the church began to demand more and more of the disciples' time, deacons were established to "wait on tables." The disciples said of their priorities:

"But we will give ourselves continually to prayer and to the ministry of the word" (Acts 6:4).

The early church members were men and women of prayer. It is recorded of them:

"And they continued steadfastly in the apostles' doctrine and fellowship, in the breaking of bread, and in prayers" (Acts 2:42).

These early believers prayed in the Temple, in their homes, and outside in nature.

"And on the Sabbath day we went out of the city to the riverside, where prayer was customarily made" (Acts 16:13).

All the apostles were men of prayer. Paul said he prayed day and night for the believers:

"Night and day praying exceedingly that we might see your face and perfect what is lacking in your faith" (1 Thess. 3:10).

Because the apostles were men of prayer, they were men of power in the Lord. The early Christians also were men and women of prayer, and God was able to do mighty wonders and miracles through them. Because of Jesus' sending of the Spirit, the gospel went to the world.

> *Because the apostles were men of prayer, they were men of power in the Lord.*

"If indeed you continue in the faith, grounded and steadfast, and are not moved away from the hope of the gospel which you heard, which was preached to every creature under heaven, of which I, Paul, became a minister" (Col. 1:23).

God calls every Christian to become a mighty prayer warrior.

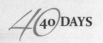

Personal Reflection and Discussion

1. Why did Jesus spend so much time in prayer?

_____

_____

2. How did Jesus' example in prayer affect the disciples?

_____

_____

3. What kind of prayer life did the early church members have?

_____

_____

4. How do you want your prayer life to change?

_____

_____

Prayer Activity

● Call your prayer partner and discuss this devotional with him/her.
● Pray with your prayer partner:
    1. for God to continue to lead each of you with His Holy Spirit.
    2. for God to lead you to become a prayer warrior as were Jesus and the disciples.
    3. for the individuals on your prayer list.

INCLUDE THE FOLLOWING BIBLE VERSE IN YOUR PRAYER:
"Let me understand the teaching of your precepts; then I will meditate on your wonders" (Ps. 119:27, NIV).

Open my understanding to Your teachings. Cause me to meditate constantly and pray continually to You.

Day 11

Why Is
Prayer Necessary?

Even though most Christians believe prayer is important, many don't understand why prayer is really necessary. Many question if God is sovereign and able to carry out His will, why do we need to pray for Him to do what He already wants and plans to do anyway? Some reason that prayer is primarily for our benefit, but God is still going to do what He wants, whether we pray or not. The idea is popular that it's a "privilege" to pray but not really a necessity for God to carry out His will on earth. The truth of the matter is that it is necessary for God's children to pray. Why else would Jesus tell us to pray that God's will be done?

"In this manner, therefore, pray: Our Father in heaven, hallowed be Your name. Your kingdom come. Your will be done on earth as it is in heaven" (Matt. 6:9, 10).

If believers do not pray, God's desires will not be carried out on this earth.

Genesis records the creation of this world and humankind:

"Then God said, 'Let Us make man in Our image, according to Our likeness; let them have dominion over the fish of the sea, over the birds of the air, and over the cattle, over all the earth and over every creeping thing that creeps on the earth.' So God created man in His own image; in the image of God He created him; male and female He created them" (Gen. 1:26, 27).

The Hebrew words translated likeness and image indicate that God created humans in many ways like Himself.

God did something else when He created man. We are told in the above verse that God gave man "dominion" over this world. The Hebrew word translated dominion means "to rule," or "reign," over. As God's representative, Adam was to be the ruler of this world:

"Then the Lord God took the man and put him in the garden of Eden to tend and keep it" (Gen. 2:15).

Adam's responsibility to "keep" the earth meant he was to protect it from anything that would do harm. Adam was to be God's authoritative representative on earth. He was to be the earth's watchman, or guardian.

The psalmist further describes the position God gave man at creation:

"For You have made him a little lower than the angels, and You have crowned him with glory and honor" (Ps. 8:5).

Looking again at the original Hebrew words translated glory and honor, we find that man was given authority similar to that of a king's reigning authority. Hence, we see that at creation the earth was put under Adam's authority. What happened on earth depended on Adam.

Prayer is necessary, because from the beginning God intended to work through humans, not independent of them, in carrying out His will on earth. God works through the prayers of His people. When God wills to do something on this earth He, at times, invites humans to participate in prayer in effecting salvation in the live of other. Many examples of this are found in both the Old and New Testaments. We are to ask that God's "will be done on earth" (Matt. 6:10). We are to ask God to "give us this day our daily bread" (verse 11).

As Jesus saw the great need of the multitudes, He asked His disciples to make the following request to the Father:

"But when He saw the multitudes, He was moved with compassion for them, because they were weary and scattered, like sheep having no shepherd. Then He said to His disciples, 'The harvest truly is plentiful, but the laborers are few. Therefore pray the Lord of the harvest to send out laborers into His harvest'" (Matt. 9:36-38).

God wants to send forth laborers into the harvest fields of this earth. However, it is necessary for Christians to ask Him to do this.

Paul asked believers to pray for the advancement of the gospel:

"Finally, brethren, pray for us, that the word of the Lord may have free course and be glorified, just as it is with you" (2 Thess. 3:1).

All of the things listed above are God's will, but it's necessary for man to pray for them because prayer releases God's power to carry out His will on this earth. Remember, it is God's plan to work through humankind, not work independent of us. Your prayers are essential for God's will to be done in your life and in the lives of those for whom you pray.

Personal Reflection and Discussion

1. Since God is "God," and has the power to do whatever He wants, isn't He going to carry out His will, whether we pray or not? Why, or why not?

_____

_____

2. What responsibility did Adam have when it came to God's will being done on earth?

_____

_____

3. Is prayer a necessity, or is it just a privilege? Why?

_____

_____

4. How do you think Satan feels about your prayer time with God?

_____

_____

Prayer Activity

- Call your prayer partner and discuss this devotional with him/her.
- Pray with your prayer partner:
  1. for God to continue to work through each of you with His Holy Spirit.
  2. for God to give you a clear understanding of the necessity of prayer.
  3. for the individuals on your prayer list.

INCLUDE THE FOLLOWING BIBLE VERSE IN YOUR PRAYER: "Keep me from deceitful ways; be gracious to me through your law" (Ps. 119:29, NIV).

Day 12

Praying in the Spirit

Every Christian is involved in warfare with the enemy with eternal consequences at stake. This battle is as real as any ever fought on this earth between nations. The battle is between the kingdom of God and the kingdom of darkness. Paul describes this battle as a wrestling match, which is up close and personal:

"For we do not wrestle against flesh and blood, but against principalities, against powers, against the rulers of the darkness of this age, against spiritual hosts of wickedness in the heavenly places" (Eph. 6:12).

We pray in the Spirit when our prayers are prompted by the Holy Spirit. We are to be directed by the Spirit as to when to pray and what to pray for.

Paul next describes the armor of God that the Christian must put on for victory. Paul concludes his description of this warfare and our defense/offense against the enemy with the words: "Praying always with all prayer and supplication in the Spirit, being watchful to this end with all perseverance and supplication for all the saints" (verse 18).

Note that Paul commands us to pray "always." We must become a prevailing prayer intercessor, praying consistently and persistently. Then he adds, "in the Spirit." Here we see that if we want victory over the enemy, praying in the Spirit is just as important as putting on the whole armor of God.

An important question, then, is What does it mean to pray in the Spirit? A brief definition would be that we pray in the Spirit when our prayers are prompted by the Holy Spirit. We are to be directed by the Spirit as to when to pray and what to pray for. The Holy Spirit is to guide us in every aspect of our prayer life. When we are praying in the Spirit, our prayers will be empowered by the Spirit. Our prayers will be effective and will bring powerful results. Hence, we can see that in order to pray in the Spirit, we must be baptized with the Spirit. Ellen White describes what it means to pray in the Spirit:

"By the Spirit every sincere prayer is indited [made up or composed], and such prayer is acceptable to God" (*The Desire of Ages,* p. 189).

Referring to Paul's statement in Romans 8:26 and 27, she writes:

"We must not only pray in Christ's name, but by the inspiration of the Holy Spirit. This explains what is meant when it is said that the Spirit 'maketh intercession for us, with groanings which cannot be uttered.' Romans 8:26. Such prayer God delights to answer" (*Christ's Object Lessons,* p. 147).

It is the Holy Spirit that calls us to prayer. He will show us some great need to pray for because God wants to begin acting in meeting that need. We read of such an experience in the case of Jesus praying for Peter:

"And the Lord said, 'Simon, Simon! Indeed, Satan has asked for you, that he may sift you as wheat. But I have prayed for you, that your faith should not fail'" (Luke 22:31, 32).

The Holy Spirit convicted Christ to pray for Peter—and even revealed what Satan's plan was concerning Peter. Once Christ knew this, He began praying for Peter. The Holy Spirit will do the same through us; He will bring to our mind someone to pray for. He may, or may not, reveal why He wants us to pray for them. The important thing is that we respond to the Spirit's prompting to pray.

Let us taste of Your mercy—lead us to confess our sins. Bring us to rejoice fully in You as we pray in the Spirit.

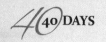

Personal Reflection and Discussion

1. In Paul's description of the spiritual warfare in which we are engaged with Satan, what did he say about prayer?

_____

_____

2. How did Ellen White describe what it means to pray in the Spirit?

_____

_____

3. Describe a time when the Holy Spirit convicted you to pray for someone.

_____

_____

4. Do you desire to be a Christian who prays in the Spirit? What steps can you take to make this a reality?

_____

_____

Prayer Activity

- **Call your prayer partner and discuss this devotional with him/her.**
- **Pray with your prayer partner:**
     1. **for God to continue to convict each of you with His Holy Spirit.**
     2. **for God to direct your prayers by the Holy Spirit.**
     3. **for the individuals on your prayer list.**

INCLUDE THE FOLLOWING BIBLE VERSE IN YOUR PRAYER: "O satisfy us early with Your mercy, that we may rejoice and be glad all our days" (Ps. 90:14).

Day 13

United Prayer in the Spirit

hristians uniting in prayer for a specific purpose has long been understood by believers to be an essential part of the Christian life. At one time I thought united prayer referred to two or more Christians coming together to pray. During prayer each one would pray for whatever came to their mind. Each prayer would have some common elements and would also have a number of requests that varied from those of the others who were praying. This is not the biblical definition for Christians uniting together in prayer. No, united prayer is two or more Christians praying for the same thing. They are united in desire, purpose, and request. They pray together at the same place and time with one prayer focus. If they cannot meet at the same place to pray, then they pray at the same time with one prayer focus, or they may pray together on the phone. However, if possible, it is more strengthening to each if they actually meet together for prayer.

In our personal lives united prayer with fellow believers is a powerful force against Satan. This is why James counsels us to join together when praying for the sick and to pray for one another:

"Is anyone among you sick? Let him call for the elders of the church, and let them pray over him, anointing him with oil in the name of the Lord. And the prayer of faith will save the sick, and the Lord will raise him up. And if he has committed sins, he will be forgiven. Confess your trespasses to one another, and pray for one another, that you may be healed. The effective, fervent prayer of a righteous man avails much" (James 5:14-16).

In fact, it is necessary for those ready to meet Jesus when He returns to have entered into genuine, united prayer for one another. We were not created to stand alone in our battle with Satan. We need one another's prayers for complete victory over the enemy.

United prayer is also essential for the advancement of God's kingdom

on this earth. Satan will resist every forward movement of God's work. United prayer will significantly increase God's power to advance His kingdom.

The Old Testament has numerous references to believers uniting together in prayer. The "teacher" in Ecclesiastes offers a significant lesson on the importance of others joining with us in our battle against our enemy, Satan:

"Though one may be overpowered, two can defend themselves. A cord of three strands is not quickly broken" (Eccl. 4:12, NIV).

Leviticus tells us:

"Five of you shall chase a hundred, and a hundred of you shall put ten thousand to flight; your enemies shall fall by the sword before you" (Lev. 26:8).

If we try to stand alone in the battle against Satan and his temptations, we will be more easily overcome. As the "teacher" says, one alone may be more easily overpowered, while two can defend themselves—and three are even stronger. This is why fellowshipping in prayer with other Christians is so important and powerful.

Jesus uttered a most significant statement about the importance—and even the necessity—of two or more believers joining together in fellowship and prayer.

"Again, I tell you that if two of you on earth agree about anything you ask for, it will be done for you by my Father in heaven. For where two or three come together in my name, there am I with them" (Matt. 18:19, 20, NIV).

When two or more believers pray in the Spirit, they can be confident that God will hear and answer their prayer:

"Now this is the confidence that we have in Him, that if we ask anything according to His will, He hears us. And if we know that He hears us, whatever we ask, we know that we have the petitions that we have asked of Him" (1 John 5:14, 15).

Cause me not to desire the things of this earth. Turn my eyes toward You. Restore my spiritual life, and help me to unite with fellow believers, especially in prayer.

Personal Reflection and Discussion

1. Describe what is meant by "united prayer in the Spirit." Why is this type of praying important?

_____

_____

2. What Scripture indicates that united prayer is even more effective than one Christian praying alone?

_____

_____

3. Why does Satan not want Christians to unite together in prayer?

_____

_____

4. What can you do to become more involved in uniting in prayer with fellow believers?

_____

_____

Prayer Activity

- **Call your prayer partner and discuss this devotional with him/her.**
- **Pray with your prayer partner:**
    1. for God to continue to lead each of you to pray in the Holy Spirit.
    2. for God to lead you to unite more often with fellow believers in prayer.
    3. for the individuals on your prayer list.

INCLUDE THE FOLLOWING BIBLE VERSE IN YOUR PRAYER: "Turn my eyes away from worthless things; preserve my life according to your word" (Ps. 119:37, NIV).

Day 14

Persevering Prayer in the Spirit

Throughout the centuries persevering prayer has been considered an essential part of the advancement of God's kingdom on earth. However, those of us who live in the Western culture tend to want quick answers to our problems. Many times this quick-fix attitude finds its way into our prayer life. Often we will pray for something occasionally, but not perseveringly. The truth is that persevering prayer is not an option; it is a necessity, just as united prayer is a necessity, if we are to be victorious over our adversary personally and corporately as a church. Those ready to meet Jesus will know from personal experience what it means to persevere in prayer. Prayer will have played a major role in preparing them for that great event.

> *Persevering prayer is not an option; it is a necessity if we are to be victorious over our adversary personally and corporately as a church.*

Jesus was personally acquainted with the necessity for persevering prayer. Many times He spent entire nights in prayer. In Luke 18 He related a story that clearly illustrated the necessity for every believer to enter into persevering prayer. Two key phrases make His point. Luke introduces the parable with these words:

"Then He spoke a parable to them, that men always ought to pray and not lose heart" (Luke 18:1).

The purpose of this parable was to teach us the necessity of persevering in prayer. Luke knew Jesus taught that we ought, or should (NIV), always pray and not faint, or stop praying, until we get the answer. The Greek form of the verb pray is continuous action. Jesus is teaching in this parable that we should keep on praying, and not stop or give up.

The second phrase that reinforces the importance of persevering prayer is this:

"And shall God not avenge His own elect who cry out day and night to Him, though He bears long with them?" (verse 7).

Here Jesus clearly teaches that many times God's answers to our prayers will come only as the result of our crying to him "day and night." Quick praying will not bring the results that consistent, persevering prayer will.

Ellen White sensed the spiritual weakness among God's people in her day. She asked God's angel why this was the case. Note the answer:

"I asked the angel why there was no more faith and power in Israel. He said: 'Ye let go of the arm of the Lord too soon. Press your petitions to the throne, and hold on by strong faith. The promises are sure. Believe ye receive the things ye ask for, and ye shall have them.' I was then pointed to Elijah. He was subject to like passions as we are, and he prayed earnestly. His faith endured the trial. Seven times he prayed before the Lord, and at last the cloud was seen" (*Early Writings,* p. 73).

Many of us still "let go of the arm of the Lord too soon." We must learn how to prevail long with the Lord in prayer.

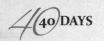

Personal Reflection and Discussion

1. What does it mean to persevere with God in prayer?

_____

_____

2. Do you think persevering prayer is easy for the average Christian in the Western world? Why, or why not?

_____

_____

3. What did Jesus say about the importance of persevering prayer?

_____

_____

4. What did the angel tell Ellen White concerning the reason there is so little power in God's church today?

_____

_____

Prayer Activity

- **Call your prayer partner and discuss this devotional with him/her.**
- **Pray with your prayer partner:**
    1. **for God to continue to bless each of you with His Holy Spirit.**
    2. **for God to lead you to learn how to persevere in prayer.**
    3. **for the individuals on your prayer list.**

INCLUDE THE FOLLOWING BIBLE VERSE IN YOUR PRAYER:
"Be joyful always; pray continually; give thanks in all circumstances, for this is God's will for you in Christ Jesus" (1 Thess. 5:16-18, NIV).

Cause us to pray to You constantly until You revive us. As we persevere in prayer, let us remember to give You thanks for the blessings You give us.

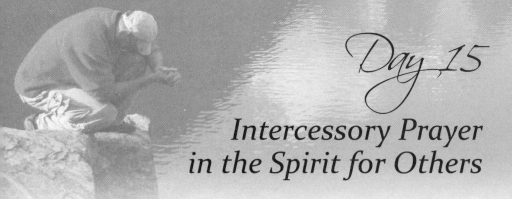

Day 15

Intercessory Prayer
in the Spirit for Others

The principle of persevering prayer applies to every area of the Christian's life, including our efforts to lead others to Christ. It should be clear from our previous discussion that our prayers are necessary for the salvation of those in our circle of family and friends.

Paul exhorts the Christian to make "intercession" for all men:

"Therefore I exhort first of all that supplications, prayers, intercessions, and giving of thanks be made for all men, for kings and all who are in authority, that we may lead a quiet and peaceable life in all godliness and reverence. For this is good and acceptable in the sight of God our Savior" (1 Tim. 2:1-3).

We are to bring about meetings with God through intercessory prayer. Our prayers for the lost bring about meetings of reconciliation between them and God and meetings of dissolution between them and Satan. Intercessory prayer is a major element in the "ministry of reconciliation" every Christian is called to participate in:

"Now all things are of God, who has reconciled us to Himself through Jesus Christ, and has given us the ministry of reconciliation, that is, that God was in Christ reconciling the world to Himself, not imputing their trespasses to them, and has committed to us the word of reconciliation" (2 Cor. 5:18, 19).

In His prayer to the Father in John 17, Christ is praying an intercessory prayer that "oneness," or "unity," take place between the Father and the believers:

"I do not pray for these alone, but also for those who will believe in Me through their word; that they all may be one, as You, Father, are in Me, and I in You; that they also may be one in Us, that the world may believe that You sent Me" (John 17:20, 21).

Christ is praying for complete reconciliation between the Father and all believers. He not only prayed that intercessory prayer for us 2,000 years ago, He continues to pray an intercessory prayer for us today:

"Therefore He is also able to save to the uttermost those who come to God through Him, since He ever lives to make intercession for them" (Heb. 7:25).

Throughout the letters of Paul we read of his continual intercession to God on behalf of those to whom he is writing (Rom. 1:9 and Eph. 1:15, 16). One such Scripture is found in Colossians 1:9:

"For this reason we also, since the day we heard it, do not cease to pray for you, and to ask that you may be filled with the knowledge of His will in all wisdom and spiritual understanding."

Paul knew them well and loved them deeply. He certainly understood the necessity of continually making intercession for all the saints. He encourages every Christian to do the same for one another:

"Praying always with all prayer and supplication in the Spirit, being watchful to this end with all perseverance and supplication for all the saints" (Eph. 6:18).

God revealed the necessity of intercessory prayer when Samuel spoke the following words to King Saul:

"Moreover, as for me, far be it from me that I should sin against the Lord in ceasing to pray for you; but I will teach you the good and the right way" (1 Sam. 12:23).

Here we learn that it is actually a sin for us to refuse to pray for one another. Ellen White encouraged prayer for one another with these words:

"Although God dwells not in temples made with hands, yet He honors with His presence the assemblies of His people. He has promised that when they come together to seek Him, to acknowledge their sins, and to pray for one another, He will meet with them by His Spirit. But those who assemble to worship Him should put away every evil thing. Unless they can worship Him in spirit and truth and in the beauty of holiness, their coming together will be of no avail" (*Review and Herald,* November 30, 1905).

As Christians are daily filled with the Spirit, God will lead in their intercessory prayer life. He will bring to their mind whom to pray for and, often, what to pray for in each person's life. Hence, we can clearly see why Satan will do everything in his power to make us believe that it is not essential or important that we specifically pray for one another. He wants us to believe that it is not really necessary for us to pray for those who are lost. He wants us to believe that God will work for the salvation of the lost even if we don't specifically pray for them. Hopefully, you will not believe his lies. This is why he will attack our prayer life, perhaps more than any other aspect of our spiritual life.

Personal Reflection and Discussion

1. When Christians intercede in prayer for someone, what are they actually doing?

_____

_____

2. How has Satan attacked your prayer life?

_____

_____

3. How can you become a more effective prayer intercessor for others?

_____

_____

Prayer Activity

- **Call your prayer partner and discuss this devotional with him/her.**
- **Pray with your prayer partner:**
    1. **for God to continue to minister to each of you with His Holy Spirit.**
    2. **for God to lead you to become an effective prayer intercessor for others.**
    3. **for the individuals on your prayer list.**

INCLUDE THE FOLLOWING BIBLE VERSE IN YOUR PRAYER:
"Then I will sprinkle clean water on you, and you shall be clean; I will cleanse you from all your filthiness and from all your idols. I will give you a new heart and put a new spirit within you; I will take the heart of stone out of your flesh and give you a heart of flesh. I will put My Spirit within you and cause you to walk in My statutes, and you will keep My judgments and do them" (Eze. 36:25-27).

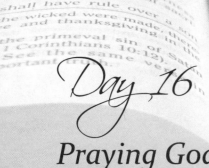

Day 16

Praying God's Promises in the Spirit

God has given us many promises in the Bible to meet our every need. Both the Old and New Testaments have outstanding examples of God's people claiming the promises of His Word when facing difficulties.

One of my first exposures to the Bible's teachings on prayer was in *The ABC's of Bible Prayer,* a book by Glenn Coon. I learned the concept of claiming God's promises in prayer as a young Christian, and it has proved to be a great blessing throughout my life and ministry. The prayer formula is simple:

Ask - "Ask, and it will be given to you; seek, and you will find; knock, and it will be opened to you" (Matt. 7:7).

Believe - "Therefore I say to you, whatever things you ask when you pray, believe that you receive them, and you will have them" (Mark 11:24).

Claim the promise with thanksgiving before any answer is seen - "And Jesus lifted up His eyes and said, 'Father, I thank You that You have heard Me. And I know that You always hear Me, but because of the people who are standing by I said this, that they may believe that You sent Me.' Now when He had said these things, He cried with a loud voice, 'Lazarus, come forth!'" (John 11:41-43).

In these verses we see that Jesus thanked the Father for hearing and answering His prayer before there was evidence of it being answered.

God's promises are sure. We can be confident that God will do what He says:

"God is not a man, that He should lie, nor a son of man, that He should repent. Has He said, and will He not do it? Or has He spoken, and will He not make it good?" (Num. 23:19).

And He can do what He promises:

"Ah, Lord God! Behold, You have made the heavens and the earth by Your great power and outstretched arm. There is nothing too hard for You" (Jer. 32:17).

Just as the oak tree is in the acorn, so is the fulfillment of God's promise in the promise itself when claimed by faith. Concerning the promises of God's Word, Ellen White writes:

"In every command and in every promise of the Word of God is the power, the very life of God, by which the command may be fulfilled and the promise realized" (*Christ's Object Lessons,* p. 38).

God's power and very life are contained in the promises of the Bible. Nothing can stand in the way of His promises being fulfilled when we claim them by faith in persevering prayer.

In 2 Chronicles 20:6-12 we find a marvelous prayer model of claiming God's promises. Jehoshaphat, king of Judah, was facing an imminent invasion by a confederacy of armies. He had made preparation for such a crisis by building up Judah's army and defenses. He had more than 1 million well-trained men ready for battle. However, when the threat became known to the king, his first response was not to look to his preparations for war, but rather look to the Lord.

When we face problems in life, our response should be the same—look to the Lord first. This doesn't mean that we don't do what we can to meet whatever situation may arise. The danger is that we have the tendency to go immediately to our human resources for help and deliverance. Our mind often begins formulating ways to solve the problem rather than turning to God first. Jehoshaphat's response is a good example for us to follow.

This prayer reveals five steps for victoriously praying for the promises of God:

1. The king began by praising God's attributes, especially those related to the problem he was facing (verse 6). He recalled that God rules over all the kingdoms of the nations, that "power and might" are in His hand, and that no one can withstand Him.

2. The king recalled past victories, similar to the present victory Judah needed (verse 7). Recalling God's provision in the past, as related to our present need, reminds us of God's faithfulness and builds our faith.

3. He stated in prayer a promise God had made to His people in the past—a promise related to the problem he was facing (verses 8, 9).

4. Jehoshaphat then stated the problem (verses 10-12).

5. He praised God before any evidence of victory was seen (verses 18, 19).

Note the formula for praying God's promises—and not focusing on the problem: praise, past victories, promise, problem, praise.

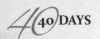

Personal Reflection and Discussion

1. Relate a time when you prayed God's promise, and how that differed from a time when you only focused on the problem in prayer.

_____

_____

2. What are the elements of King Jehoshaphat's prayer? Which elements do you struggle with implementing in your prayer life?

_____

_____

3. List your favorite promises from God's Word.

_____

_____

Prayer Activity

- Call your prayer partner and discuss this devotional with him/her.
- Pray with your prayer partner:
    1. for God to continue to fill each of you with His Holy Spirit.
    2. for God to lead you to learn how to pray His promises rather than focusing on the problems you face.
    3. for the individuals on your prayer list.

INCLUDE THE FOLLOWING BIBLE VERSE IN YOUR PRAYER:
"Give me understanding, and I will keep your law and obey it with all my heart" (Ps. 119:34, NIV).

Give me the desire to obey You with all my heart.
Help me to focus on You and Your promises
instead of my problems.

Day 17

Gospel Work Finished Under Holy Spirit Power

J esus foretold that the "gospel of the kingdom will be preached in all the world as a witness to all the nations, and then the end will come" (Matt. 24:14). Just before Jesus comes there will be a tremendous evangelism explosion that will produce a mighty witness of the gospel on this earth.

The prophet Joel foretold two great Holy Spirit outpourings—the former, or early, rain and latter rain:

"Be glad then, you children of Zion, and rejoice in the Lord your God; for He has given you the former rain faithfully, and He will cause the rain to come down for you—the former rain, and the latter rain in the first month" (Joel 2:23).

Peter indicated in his sermon on the day of Pentecost that the outpouring of the Holy Spirit had begun on that day:

"But this is what was spoken by the prophet Joel: 'And it shall come to pass in the last days, says God, that I will pour out of My Spirit on all flesh; your sons and your daughters shall prophesy, your young men shall see visions, your old men shall dream dreams. And on My menservants and on My maidservants I will pour out My Spirit in those days; and they shall prophesy'" (Acts 2:16-18).

This early rain of the Spirit is also called the baptism of the Holy Spirit:

"And being assembled together with them, He commanded them not to depart from Jerusalem, but to wait for the Promise of the Father, 'which,' He said, 'you have heard from Me; for John truly baptized with water, but you shall be baptized with the Holy Spirit not many days from now.' . . . 'But you shall receive power when the Holy Spirit has come upon you; and you shall be witnesses to Me in Jerusalem, and in all Judea and Samaria, and to the end of the earth'" (Acts 1:4-8).

The book of Acts describes the great evangelism explosion that took place at that time. Thousands were won to Christ.

Every Christian who has read the book of Acts has probably longed for the day that a similar mighty working of the Holy Spirit will take place again. Several years ago I started to better understand how the mighty moving of God's Spirit will happen as I began studying and seeking the baptism of the Holy Spirit.

God began clarifying how "anointed, Spirit-filled" believers will be mightily used by Him to win thousands to Christ. I realized that the professional evangelist and radio or television broadcasts would not finish God's last-day work, though these will play a role. Rather, God's work will be finished when His people seek and experience the baptism of the Holy Spirit and allow Christ to reach out to others through them. God's work will not be finished by some new program or method; God will finish His work through Spirit-filled believers who surrender themselves completely to Christ and allow Him to live in them and minister to others through them. That is why Jesus told the disciples to wait for the baptism of the Holy Spirit before they sought to take the gospel to the world (Acts 1:4-8). Even though they had been with Jesus and ministered to others for three and one half years, they weren't yet ready to tell the world about Jesus. They needed to wait for the power of the Spirit.

> *God will finish His work through Spirit-filled believers who surrender themselves completely to Christ and allow Him to live in them and minister to others through them.*

When consecrated Christians experience Christ in this way, the second great evangelism explosion will take place, and the second great outpouring of the Holy Spirit, called the latter rain, will fall upon this earth. This section of these devotional studies is dedicated to helping the reader understand how this second great evangelism explosion will take place, and how every believer can be a part of it. In fact, all who are ready to meet Jesus when He returns will have had a part in it.

Personal Reflection and Discussion

1. Have you experienced the power of the Holy Spirit as much as you would like in witnessing to others? Expand on your answer.

_____

_____

2. What do you think will be the major factor in God's work being finished?

_____

_____

3. How can you become part of this last evangelistic work of God?

_____

_____

Prayer Activity

● Call your prayer partner and discuss this devotional with him/her.
● Pray with your prayer partner:
   1. for God to continue to anoint each of you with His Holy Spirit.
   2. for God to lead you to learn how you can become an effective witness for Jesus.
   3. for God to pour out the latter rain of the Holy Spirit.
   4. for the individuals on your prayer list.

INCLUDE THE FOLLOWING BIBLE VERSE IN YOUR PRAYER:
"O Lord, I have heard Your speech and was afraid; O Lord, revive Your work in the midst of the years! In the midst of the years make it known; in wrath remember mercy" (Hab. 3:2).

Lead us from our sin; have mercy on us and forgive us. Glorify Your name through great works of salvation. Prepare us for the latter rain, and pour out your Spirit that the work may be finished.

Day 18

The Holy Spirit and Witnessing

Seventh-day Adventists, as well as many other Christians, have been anticipating the second coming of Christ for many years. The parable of the 10 virgins teaches that the Bridegroom's return would be delayed.

What is at the heart of this delay in Christ's return? I believe there are two reasons. First, God's people are not ready. Second, the work of preaching the gospel to the world, warning them of Christ's coming and the events surrounding that event, hasn't happened. The three angels' messages of Revelation chapter 14 haven't gone to the world, as they must before Christ returns:

"Then I saw another angel flying in the midst of heaven, having the everlasting gospel to preach to those who dwell on the earth—to every nation, tribe, tongue, and people—saying with a loud voice, 'Fear God and give glory to Him, for the hour of His judgment has come; and worship Him who made heaven and earth, the sea and springs of water.' And another angel followed, saying, 'Babylon is fallen, is fallen, that great city, because she has made all nations drink of the wine of the wrath of her fornication.' Then a third angel followed them, saying with a loud voice, 'If anyone worships the beast and his image, and receives his mark on his forehead or on his hand, he himself shall also drink of the wine of the wrath of God, which is poured out full strength into the cup of His indignation. And he shall be tormented with fire and brimstone in the presence of the holy angels and in the presence of the Lamb. And the smoke of their torment ascends forever and ever; and they have no rest day or night, who worship the beast and his image, and whoever receives the mark of his name.' Here is the patience of the saints; here are those who keep the commandments of God and the faith of Jesus. Then I heard a voice from heaven saying to me, 'Write: "Blessed are the dead who die in the Lord from now on."' 'Yes,' says the Spirit, 'that they may rest from their labors, and their works follow them.' And I looked, and behold, a white cloud, and on the cloud sat One like the Son of Man, having on His head a golden crown, and in His hand a sharp sickle" (Rev. 14:6-14).

Great and terrible events are to come upon this earth just prior to Christ's second coming. In the past God's people have not been ready for such events, as in Noah's day when the Flood didn't come until the warning of the Flood had gone out to earth's inhabitants, and the boat was ready for the Deluge (Matt. 24:37). The warning message will be given and the "boat," or church, will be ready. Then the end will come.

How did Christ get the most serious message of Noah to the world of Noah's day? Peter tells us in his first letter. The Holy Spirit that "quickened" Christ, or raised Him from the grave, is the Spirit by which Christ "preached" through Noah to men and women (called spirits) who were captives, or prisoners, of Satan:

"For Christ also suffered once for sins, the just for the unjust, that He might bring us to God, being put to death in the flesh but made alive by the Spirit, by whom also He went and preached to the spirits in prison, who formerly were disobedient, when once the longsuffering of God waited in the days of Noah, while the ark was being prepared, in which a few, that is, eight souls, were saved through water" (1 Peter 3:18-20).

Numbers 27:15 and 16 indicates that the Bible uses the word spirits to refer to living men and women. The Bible also indicates that the term prison, or prisoners, can refer to men and women under Satan's power of sin and deception (Isa. 42:6, 7).

Hence, we see from Scripture that it was Christ, by the Holy Spirit, speaking through Noah, who prepared the inhabitants of the earth for the Flood. So it will be in the last days just before Christ's second coming (Matt. 24:37). Christ will speak by the Holy Spirit through Spirit-filled Christians to prepare the world for the Second Advent.

I have been a Seventh-day Adventist Christian for many years, and a pastor for most of those years. In my denomination, as well as in many other Christian organizations, I believe much time and money has been spent on plans, programs, and methods to bring Christ to the world. I'm not against plans, programs, and methods, but I'm afraid that we have, more often than not, depended on these things to finish God's work. Plans, programs, and methods will not finish God's work. Great speakers, marvelous Christian musical concerts, or satellites will not finish God's work. God's Holy Spirit will finish God's work—God's Spirit, speaking and ministering through Spirit-filled men and women.

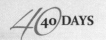

Personal Reflection and Discussion

1. Why do you think Jesus has not come yet?

_____

_____

2. What comparison did Jesus make between the time of Noah and our day?

_____

_____

3. What, or whom, do you think God will use most in finishing His work on earth?

_____

_____

4. What can you do to become one whom God will use to finish His work?

_____

_____

Prayer Activity

- Call your prayer partner and discuss this devotional with him/her.
- Pray with your prayer partner:
    1. for God to continue to draw each of you into a closer walk with Jesus with His Holy Spirit.
    2. for God to witness through you by His Spirit, as He did through Noah.
    3. for the individuals on your prayer list.

INCLUDE THE FOLLOWING BIBLE VERSE IN YOUR PRAYER:
"Direct me in the path of your commands, for there I find delight" (Ps. 119:35, NIV).

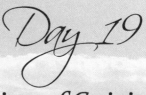

The Necessity of Spirit Baptism in Witnessing

The necessity of the baptism of the Holy Spirit for witnessing is clearly revealed in the New Testament. We see it in the experience of Jesus.

Luke says that from that time forward Jesus was "filled" with the Holy Spirit and ministered in the "power" of the Spirit.

"The Spirit of the Lord is upon Me, because He has annointed Me to preach the gospel to the poor; He has sent Me to heal the brokenhearted, to proclaim liberty to the captives and recovery of sight to the blind, to set at liberty those who are oppressed, to proclaim the acceptable year of the Lord" (Luke 4:18, 19).

"God anointed Jesus of Nazareth with the Holy Spirit and with power, who went about doing good and healing all who were oppressed by the devil, for God was with Him" (Acts 10:38).

Jesus knew the importance and necessity of Spirit-filled ministry. This is why He told the disciples to wait for the promise of the baptism of the Holy Spirit before they went forth to proclaim the gospel (Acts 1:4, 5). Jesus went on to tell them that they would receive power to witness when they received the baptism of the Holy Spirit (verse 8).

The disciples did what Jesus asked them to do. They waited and united in prayer for the promise of the baptism of the Holy Spirit to be fulfilled to them (verse 14).

In answer to their 10 days of praying, the Holy Spirit came on the day of Pentecost and "they were all filled with the Holy Spirit" (Acts 2:1-4).

What happened next reveals one of the main purposes for the baptism of the Holy Spirit. God used these Spirit-filled believers to tell of the "wonderful works of God" (verses 7-11). God even surmounted language barriers to share the good news of a risen Savior to the Jews who were present on that day. Three thousand responded to Peter's Spirit-empowered sermon (verse 41) and the early church continued to grow (verse 47).

These early Christians recognized the urgency of receiving the baptism of the Holy Spirit in order to live a godly life and effectively witness for their Lord. Spirit baptism was so important that when many Samaritan men and women accepted Jesus as their Savior and were baptized in water under Philip's ministry, Peter and John were sent to meet with them, lay hands on them, and pray for the baptism of the Holy Spirit (Acts 8:12-17).

We see the same priority in God's call to Saul on the road to Damascus. Christ revealed Himself to Saul in a vision:

"As he journeyed he came near Damascus, and suddenly a light shone around him from heaven. Then he fell to the ground, and heard a voice saying to him, 'Saul, Saul, why are you persecuting Me?' And he said, 'Who are You, Lord?' Then the Lord said, 'I am Jesus, whom you are persecuting. It is hard for you to kick against the goads.' So he, trembling and astonished, said, 'Lord, what do You want me to do?' Then the Lord said to him, 'Arise and go into the city, and you will be told what you must do.' And the men who journeyed with him stood speechless, hearing a voice but seeing no one" (Acts 9:3-7).

> *Spiritual strength and power for witnessing resulted from the baptism of the Holy Spirit Saul received when Ananias prayed for him.*

Then Christ directed Saul to go to Damascus and wait for further instruction, after which God sent Ananias to Saul to lay hands on him and pray that he might receive his sight and be filled with the Holy Spirit:

"And Ananias went his way and entered the house; and laying his hands on him he said, 'Brother Saul, the Lord Jesus, who appeared to you on the road as you came, has sent me that you may receive your sight and be filled with the Holy Spirit.' Immediately there fell from his eyes something like scales, and he received his sight at once; and he arose and was baptized" (verses 17, 18).

As a result of the Spirit's infilling, "Saul increased all the more in strength" (verse 22). The word strength is not simply referring to physical strength. The context indicates that Saul increased in spiritual strength and power in proclaiming the gospel. This spiritual strength and power for witnessing resulted from the baptism of the Holy Spirit Saul received when Ananias prayed for him.

Personal Reflection and Discussion

1. When did Jesus' service for His Father become powerful, and how does the Bible describe His Spirit-filled ministry?

_____

_____

2. What did Jesus tell the disciples to do before they began ministering?

_____

_____

3. What results did the early church have after they received the baptism of the Holy Spirit?

_____

_____

Prayer Activity

- Call your prayer partner and discuss this devotional with him/her.
- Pray with your prayer partner:
  1. for God to continue to fill each of you with His Holy Spirit.
  2. for God to witness through you in the power of the Spirit, as He did in the early church.
  3. for the individuals on your prayer list.

INCLUDE THE FOLLOWING BIBLE VERSE IN YOUR PRAYER:
"I am laid low in the dust; preserve my life according to your word" (Ps. 119:25, NIV).

We are far from where we should be spiritually. Restore us spiritually as You have promised. Give us strength that we might be witnesses for You.

Day 20

Spirit Baptism and Preparing the Way for Christ's Advent

The prophet Malachi foretold that God would send Elijah, referring to an "Elijah message," just prior to the coming of Jesus Christ:

"Behold, I will send you Elijah the prophet before the coming of the great and dreadful day of the Lord" (Mal. 4:5).

This prophecy has two applications. One applies to Christ's first advent; the other applies to His second coming.

The gospel writer Luke tells us that John the Baptist fulfilled the first application of this prophecy of Malachi:

"He will also go before Him in the spirit and power of Elijah, 'to turn the hearts of the fathers to the children,' and the disobedient to the wisdom of the just, to make ready a people prepared for the Lord" (Luke 1:17).

John the Baptist went forward in ministry in the "spirit and power" of Elijah. To what did this refer? It meant that he was Spirit-filled and preached a Spirit-anointed message to prepare the people of his day for the Messiah, who would soon appear:

"For he will be great in the sight of the Lord, and shall drink neither wine nor strong drink. He will also be filled with the Holy Spirit, even from his mother's womb" (Luke 1:15).

The power of the Holy Spirit attended John's preaching. Multitudes came to hear him, and many were baptized:

"In those days John the Baptist came preaching in the wilderness of Judea, and saying, 'Repent, for the kingdom of heaven is at hand!' For this is he who was spoken of by the prophet Isaiah, saying: 'The voice of one crying in the wilderness: "Prepare the way of the Lord; make His paths straight."' Now John himself was clothed in camel's hair, with a leather belt around his waist; and his food was locusts and wild honey. Then Jerusalem, all Judea, and all the region around the Jordan went out to him and were baptized by him in the Jordan, confessing their sins" (Matt. 3:1-6).

Jesus was well aware of Malachi's prophecy, and He applied it to the mission and message of John the Baptist:

"For all the prophets and the law prophesied until John. And if you are willing to receive it, he is Elijah who is to come. He who has ears to hear, let him hear!" (Matt. 11:13-15).

Malachi's prophecy has a second application, referring to a people who will give a serious warning message just before Jesus comes, which is called the three angels' messages (Rev. 14:6-12).

This last-day Elijah message is intended to prepare men and women for Christ's second coming. As John the Baptist had to be Spirit-filled to give the Elijah message of his day, so God's last-day believers must be Spirit-filled to give the last-day Elijah message to the world today. This last-day message of warning that will be given by a Spirit-filled people will go forth in the "spirit and power" of Elijah, as did John's message.

We have not yet tapped into the mighty blessing and power that awaits us when God's people become a Spirit-filled people.

Why hasn't this final message yet been given with such power? It has been preached for more than 150 years. Millions of dollars have been, and are being, spent to give it. What's wrong? I personally believe our lack of understanding and experiencing the baptism of the Holy Spirit is the answer. I don't mean that God has not blessed our efforts to warn the world of Christ's second coming and the issues involved in these last days. I am saying that we have not yet tapped into the mighty blessing and power that awaits us when God's people become a Spirit-filled people. When that happens the last-day message of Elijah will go forth in the "spirit and power" of Elijah.

Personal Reflection and Discussion

1. What are the two applications of Malachi's prophecy about Elijah?

_____

_____

2. What is the Elijah message for today?

_____

_____

3. What spiritual experience is necessary for the second application of Malachi's prophecy to be fulfilled?

_____

_____

4. What will happen when God's last message is given in the "spirit and power" of Elijah?

_____

_____

Prayer Activity

● Call your prayer partner and discuss this devotional with him/her.
● Pray with your prayer partner:
    1. for God to continue to anoint each of you with His Holy Spirit.
    2. for God to lead His people and church to become Spirit-filled.
    3. for the individuals on your prayer list.

INCLUDE THE FOLLOWING BIBLE VERSE IN YOUR PRAYER:
"Turn my heart toward your statutes and not toward selfish gain"
(Ps. 119:36, NIV).

Cause me to love Your counsels, and turn me from the love of money and position. Fill me with Your Spirit that I might be as strong as Elijah.

Day 21

The Church's
Laodicean Problem

God gave a prophetic history of the Christian church in the book of Revelation. Revelation 2 and 3 describe seven eras of church history that apply to seven literal churches in Asia. They also apply to seven historical eras of the church, from the early apostolic church to today.

The seventh church is described in Revelation 3:14-21:

"And to the angel of the church of the Laodiceans write, 'These things says the Amen, the Faithful and True Witness, the Beginning of the creation of God: "I know your works, that you are neither cold nor hot. I could wish you were cold or hot. So then, because you are lukewarm, and neither cold nor hot, I will spew you out of My mouth. Because you say, 'I am rich, have become wealthy, and have need of nothing'—and do not know that you are wretched, miserable, poor, blind, and naked—I counsel you to buy from Me gold refined in the fire, that you may be rich; and white garments, that you may be clothed, that the shame of your nakedness may not be revealed; and anoint your eyes with eye salve, that you may see. As many as I love, I rebuke and chasten. Therefore be zealous and repent. Behold, I stand at the door and knock. If anyone hears My voice and opens the door, I will come in to him and dine with him, and he with Me. To him who overcomes I will grant to sit with Me on My throne, as I also overcame and sat down with My Father on His throne." ' "

Today's church era is called Laodicea. The city of Laodicea was known for its therapeutic hot and cold hydrotherapy baths. The benefits of hydrotherapy are well understood today, and this is significant when we consider that God describes today's church as lukewarm, and neither hot nor cold (verse 16). This displeases God very much, so much so that if the church remains in this lukewarm condition, God will spew her out of His mouth.

Why is this lukewarm condition so serious in God's sight? The answer is seen in His desire for the church. God desires that the church be either hot or cold—He desires the church to be of "therapeutic" value on this earth. You see, a lukewarm church is not therapeutic—it offers little benefit to those who come in contact with it. God wants the church to bring life everywhere it goes.

This is similar to Jesus' statement that the church is to be the "salt of the earth":

"You are the salt of the earth; but if the salt loses its flavor, how shall it be seasoned? It is then good for nothing but to be thrown out and trampled underfoot by men" (Matt. 5:13).

Both salt and hot-and-cold hydrotherapy are therapeutic. Jesus said in Revelation that those remaining in a lukewarm, nontherapeutic condition will be spewed out of His mouth. In Matthew He says that salt that "loses its flavor" will be "thrown out" (5:13). Jesus is saying the same thing in both Revelation and Matthew. If the church is not therapeutic, it is of no value to God and will ultimately be cast from Him.

God desires that the church be either hot or cold.

Jesus revealed how life was to flow from His church when He said, "He who believes in Me, as the Scripture has said, out of his heart will flow rivers of living water." John interpreted what Jesus meant this way: "But this He spoke concerning the Spirit, whom those believing in Him would receive; for the Holy Spirit was not yet given, because Jesus was not yet glorified" (John 7:38, 39). Through the baptism of the Holy Spirit life would flow from the church.

We can clearly see that God's warning to last-day Laodicean Christians is very serious. We must wake up to our condition and allow God to change us from nontherapeutic to therapeutic if we are to be ready to meet Jesus when He comes. The sad truth is that Laodicean Christians are not even aware of their dangerous spiritual condition:

"Because you say, 'I am rich, have become wealthy, and have need of nothing'—and do not know that you are wretched, miserable, poor, blind, and naked" (Rev. 3:17).

Personal Reflection and Discussion

1. Why does God want the church to be either hot or cold? What does the Bible mean when God says the church today is lukewarm?

_____

_____

2. What do you think are evidences that a local congregation may be lukewarm?

_____

_____

3. What do you think may be evidence that you are a lukewarm Adventist?

_____

_____

Prayer Activity

- Call your prayer partner and discuss this devotional with him/her.
- Pray with your prayer partner:
    1. for God to continue to baptize each of you with His Holy Spirit.
    2. for God to bring His church out of her lukewarm, Laodicean condition.
    3. for the individuals on your prayer list.

INCLUDE THE FOLLOWING BIBLE VERSE IN YOUR PRAYER:
"Turn Yourself to me, and have mercy on me, for I am desolate and afflicted. The troubles of my heart have enlarged; oh, bring me out of my distresses! Look on my affliction and my pain, and forgive all my sins" (Ps. 25:16-18).

Have mercy upon us for we are spiritually desolate and afflicted. Forgive us our sins and bring us out of our Laodicean condition.

Day 22

The Solution to the Church's Laodicean Condition

A very important question for the church today is How can we be changed from "nontherapeutic" to "therapeutic"? God's message to the Laodiceans gives us the answer. Jesus says He is standing at the door and wants into our lives:

"Behold, I stand at the door, and knock: if anyone hears My voice and opens the door, I will come in to him and dine with him, and he with Me" (Rev. 3:20).

How do we let Him in? By becoming zealous and repenting (Rev. 3:19b).

In these verses Jesus tells the disciples that He would come to them when the Holy Spirit was available to live in them. This took place on the day of Pentecost. It is through the baptism of the Holy Spirit that Jesus lives in the believer:

"Now he who keeps His commandments abides in Him, and He in him. And by this we know that He abides in us, by the Spirit whom He has given us" (1 John 3:24).

What will the baptism of the Holy Spirit do for a lukewarm Christian? The infilling of God's Spirit will bring revival to the recipient, and revival is the only answer to Laodicea's problem. Only by revival will the church become therapeutic to this world. Only by revival will the church come to a spiritual condition such that God can use her in a mighty way as a means of delivering men and women from the powers of darkness.

Ellen White knew the importance and urgency of revival when she wrote:

"A revival of true godliness among us is the greatest and most urgent of all our needs. To seek this should be our first work" (*Selected Messages,* book 1, p. 121).

She also understood the relationship between receiving the baptism of the Holy Spirit and revival:

"The baptism of the Holy Ghost as on the day of Pentecost will lead to a revival of true religion and to the performance of many wonderful works" (*Selected Messages,* book 2, p. 57).

The baptism of the Holy Spirit gives the Laodicean Christian the power needed to be revived spiritually, and also the power for witnessing. Jesus certainly knew the importance of what would happen when the Holy Spirit would be poured out in early-rain power on the day of Pentecost. Speaking of this, He said:

"I have come to bring fire on the earth, and how I wish it were already kindled!" (Luke 12:49, NIV).

What fire was Jesus speaking of? The fire of the Holy Spirit:

"John answered, saying to them all, 'I indeed baptize you with water; but One mightier than I is coming, whose sandal strap I am not worthy to loose. He will baptize you with the Holy Spirit and with fire'" (Luke 3:16).

How does the Laodicean Christian receive the baptism of the Holy Spirit and experience revival? The same way believers always have—by prayerfully claiming God's promise. The baptism of the Holy Spirit was received by the early church on the day of Pentecost as a result of their united prayers. For 10 days they claimed Christ's promise:

"And being assembled together with them, He commanded them not to depart from Jerusalem, but to wait for the Promise of the Father, 'which,' He said, 'you have heard from Me; for John truly baptized with water, but you shall be baptized with the Holy Spirit not many days from now'" (Acts 1:4, 5). "But you shall receive power when the Holy Spirit has come upon you; and you shall be witnesses to Me in Jerusalem, and in all Judea and Samaria, and to the end of the earth" (verse 8). "These all continued with one accord in prayer and supplication, with the women and Mary the mother of Jesus, and with His brothers" (verse 14).

Ellen White confirmed this:

"A revival need be expected only in answer to prayer" (*Selected Messages,* book 1, p. 121).

Every Christian today needs to pray the prayer of David: "Will You not revive us again, that Your people may rejoice in You?" (Ps. 85:6).

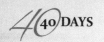

Personal Reflection and Discussion

1. What is the only solution to the Laodicean problem?

_____

_____

2. What does Ellen White say is the greatest need of the church?

_____

_____

3. What two things must the church do in order to experience genuine revival?

_____

_____

4. What do you think will be seen in the life of a Spirit-filled, revived Adventist church and Adventist member?

_____

_____

Prayer Activity

- Call your prayer partner and discuss this devotional with him/her.
- Pray with your prayer partner:
    1. for God to continue to fill each of you with His Holy Spirit.
    2. for God to bring revival into your life and His church.
    3. for the individuals on your prayer list.

INCLUDE THE FOLLOWING BIBLE VERSE IN YOUR PRAYER:
"Will You not revive us again, that Your people may rejoice in You?"
(Ps. 85:6).

Revive us and make us a people who rejoice in You.
Fill us so that we may be on fire for You.

Day 23

Prayer and Evangelism

As we learned yesterday, God's Word teaches that prayer is necessary for an individual and a church to experience revival. Prayer is necessary for the "strongholds" of Satan to be cast down, and for the saving of the lost:

"For the weapons of our warfare are not carnal but mighty in God for pulling down strongholds, casting down arguments and every high thing that exalts itself against the knowledge of God, bringing every thought into captivity to the obedience of Christ" (2 Cor. 10:4, 5).

Prayer is necessary for a Christian to remain strong in the Lord:

"Praying always with all prayer and supplication in the Spirit, being watchful to this end with all perseverance and supplication for all the saints" (Eph. 6:18).

I find it amazing that prayer, which seems so powerless and insignificant to the natural person, is so necessary and powerful for the spiritual person. Why is prayer so important and necessary in God's work?

Those who we know are outside of Christ and living under Satan's power are in a very dangerous position. Their eternal destiny is in jeopardy if they don't change. Yet of themselves they are powerless to change. Paul describes them as those whose minds have been blinded by Satan:

"But even if our gospel is veiled, it is veiled to those who are perishing, whose minds the god of this age has blinded, who do not believe, lest the light of the gospel of the glory of Christ, who is the image of God, should shine on them" (2 Cor. 4:3, 4).

The lost are blinded to the gospel because it is "hid" from their view. The word translated hid is the Greek word kalupsis, which refers to a "veil." The key to saving the lost is to remove this veil that blinds them. By adding the prefix apo to the Greek word for veil the word becomes "revelation,"

or "unveiling." Hence, the lost need an unveiling, or a revelation of God's truth. The lost don't need more information—they need an unveiling of their understanding so they can "see" the truth of the gospel. An important question, then, is How can this unveiling happen in the lives of the lost?

Intercessory prayer will remove from the mind of the unbeliever the veil causing spiritual blindness. Satan has false imaginations, or thoughts and strongholds, well established in the minds of the lost. The good news is that God has given the Christian the authority to pull down Satan's strongholds and to bring "every thought into captivity to the obedience of Christ" (2 Cor. 10:5). These two verses are very important when it comes to understanding the place of intercessory prayer for the lost. Ellen White clearly understood the necessity of prayer for those outside of Christ when she wrote:

> *Intercessory prayer will remove from the mind of the unbeliever the veil causing spiritual blindness.*

"Through much prayer you must labor for souls, for this is the only method by which you can reach hearts. It is not your work, but the work of Christ who is by your side, that impresses hearts" (*Evangelism*, p. 342).

The *Praying Church Sourcebook* gives the following list of what God's will is for the unsaved. As believers in Christ we have the right to press these requests before the throne of grace on behalf of the lost. Include in your prayer the following:

1. That God will draw them to Himself (John 6:44)
2. That they seek to know God (Acts 17:27)
3. That they believe the Word of God (1 Thess. 2:13)
4. That Satan be bound from blinding them to the truth and his influences in their life be cast down (2 Cor. 4:4; 10:4, 5)
5. That the Holy Spirit work in them (John 16:8-13)
6. That they turn from sin (Acts 3:19)
7. That they believe in Christ as Savior (John 1:12)
8. That they obey Christ as Lord (Matt. 7:21)
9. That they take root and grow in Christ (Col. 2:6, 7)

Personal Reflection and Discussion

1. What does Ellen White say about praying for the lost?

_____

_____

2. What does prayer do for those we are witnessing to?

_____

_____

3. How do you plan to apply the principles of prayer for those on your prayer list?

_____

_____

Prayer Activity

- Call your prayer partner and discuss this devotional with him/her.
- Pray with your prayer partner:
    1. for God to continue to anoint each of you with His Holy Spirit.
    2. for God to bring revival into your life and His church.
    3. for God to lead you to become a true prayer warrior for the lost.
    4. for the individuals on your prayer list.

INCLUDE THE FOLLOWING BIBLE VERSE IN YOUR PRAYER:
"And let the beauty of the Lord our God be upon us, and establish the work of our hands for us; yes, establish the work of our hands" (Ps. 90:17).

May Your character be seen in our lives. Bless our efforts to advance Your kingdom in this congregation and our community.

Day 24

Christ's Method of Evangelism

Ellen White gave us a very clear description of Christ's witnessing method:

"The Saviour mingled with men as one who desired their good. He showed His sympathy for them, ministered to their needs, and won their confidence. Then He bade them, 'Follow Me'" (*Ministry of Healing,* p. 143).

Since this was Christ's method of witnessing, when we receive the baptism of the Holy Spirit and Christ begins living more fully in us, He will begin seeking to manifest this method of witnessing through us. He will begin leading us to "mingle" with those in our circle of family and friends, putting in our heart a desire "for their good." The greatest good is for them to come to know Jesus Christ as their Savior.

Christ's method was to take the initiative in contacting those around Him. He wants you and me to do the same. If you find this difficult you need to continue to pray for the Lord to help you with this, and He will! Remember, it is Jesus in you who prompts you to do this. As you continue to yield yourself to His control in every area of your life, your witnessing will become more and more like His method.

When we continue to pray for the baptism of the Holy Spirit, more and more of the love of God will be manifested in our hearts:

"Now hope does not disappoint, because the love of God has been poured out in our hearts by the Holy Spirit who was given to us" (Rom. 5:5).

This love will be seen in our ministry to others. They will begin to gain confidence that we really do care for them and will be willing to share with us the things that concern them. Everyone has hurts, disappointed dreams, frustrations, and problems with which they are struggling. This is the very reason Christ has led you to them. He knows their needs, and knows that you have the answer for them. Christ wants to reveal that answer through you to them. He wants to reveal Himself to them through you. Ellen White wrote concerning this:

"Christian sociability is altogether too little cultivated by God's people. . . . Especially should those who have tasted the love of Christ develop their social powers, for in this way they may win souls to the Saviour" (*Testimonies for the Church,* vol. 6, p. 172).

"So it is through personal contact and association that men are reached by the saving power of the gospel" (*Thoughts From the Mount of Blessing,* p. 36).

How does this all apply to the Spirit-filled Christian? First, pray for Christ to continue to fill you with His Spirit and give you the passion for souls that He has. Make a list of those in your circle of family and friends who you feel do not know Christ, or who may be a Christian but do not know the important message of Christ's second coming. Begin praying for these individuals every day, applying the prayer principles listed in the previous devotional. Next, pray that God will provide the opportunity for you to begin coming close to them to help them in some way. We must be willing to invest the time and energy it takes to come close to people. Our interest in them must be genuine, truly caring for them and wanting to help them. When in contact with those you are praying for, look for the openings God gives you to share with them.

Always remember that God is already seeking to draw their minds and interests to Himself. In many cases He just needs us to make ourselves available for Him to speak a word of encouragement to them. God will give you the words to speak. He knows what they need to hear, and Holy Spirit power will attend the words you speak.

Bless Your Word that has been preached and taught to this congregation. Bless the words that I speak as I witness for You. May Your Word accomplish the purpose for which You sent it.

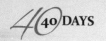
Personal Reflection and Discussion

1. List the elements of Christ's witnessing method.

_____

_____

2. Why do you think Christ chose this method for witnessing?

_____

_____

3. What should Christians do if they don't have the desire to witness for Christ?

_____

_____

4. What specifically should the Christian ask God to do in relation to witnessing?

_____

_____

5. How do you plan to apply Christ's witnessing method?

_____

_____

Prayer Activity

- **Call your prayer partner and discuss this devotional with him/her.**
- **Pray with your prayer partner:**
    1. for God to continue to baptize each of you with His Holy Spirit.
    2. for God to bring revival into your life and His church.
    3. for God to lead you to witness as Christ witnessed to others.
    4. for the individuals on your prayer list.

INCLUDE THE FOLLOWING BIBLE VERSE IN YOUR PRAYER:
"So is my word that goes out from my mouth: it will not return to me empty, but will accomplish what I desire and achieve the purpose for which I sent it" (Isa. 55:11, NIV).

Day 25

The Path to Discovery

The abiding-in-Christ teaching in the Bible is one of the most important truths that a Christian can understand. Everything hinges on experiencing the reality of abiding in Christ and Christ abiding in the believer. However, every Christian who discovers this glorious truth of Christ in us has followed a similar path as their fellow travelers. They had accepted Christ as their Savior but were burdened and bewildered by their Christian walk that was so sporadic in obedience and unfruitful in service. They longed for a consistently faithful walk with their Lord, but never found it. They struggled with besetting sins, but the sins seemed to win the battle. They prayed and studied their Bibles, but that didn't seem to bring the victory they longed for. After perhaps years of struggle, they came to the point of despair and weariness. Their sense of failure was overwhelming. The life of continual victory over sin seemed impossible to attain.

Then one day they discovered the reality of the mystery of union with Christ—Christ living in them. Once discovered, they were amazed at how simple this marvelous truth is, yet it had eluded their understanding for years. After this discovery their life was never again the same. Their joy in the Lord was deep and abiding. Their life was now consistently victorious, even over besetting sins. They no longer felt burdened or anxious in their service for the Lord, and their service became the most fruitful.

The truth of abiding in Christ and His abiding in us, and how we are to experience a victorious Christian life is so simple—and yet so elusive—that most Christians have never discovered it to the fullest. Today God is calling us to this amazing experience in Christ. Why? Jesus is coming soon! All who are ready to meet Him will be just like Him:

"Beloved, now we are children of God; and it has not yet been revealed

what we shall be, but we know that when He is revealed, we shall be like Him, for we shall see Him as He is" (1 John 3:2).

Their daily experience will become one of complete victory in Christ:

"For to this you were called, because Christ also suffered for us, leaving us an example, that you should follow His steps: 'Who committed no sin, nor was guile found in His mouth'; who, when He was reviled, did not revile in return; when He suffered, He did not threaten, but committed Himself to Him who judges righteously" (1 Peter 2:21-23).

Therefore, this wonderful biblical truth is of no small consequence to Christians living in our day. Jesus is coming soon, and God is calling us to a much higher experience with Him than most of us have ever had. This devotional section is dedicated to the goal of leading all who read it to understand and experience the abiding God is offering to us; Christ in us, the hope of glory for His people:

"To them God willed to make known what are the riches of the glory of this mystery among the Gentiles: which is Christ in you, the hope of glory" (Col. 1:27).

When this truth is understood and discovered, the believer will proclaim from the depths of his heart, "Christ did it all." The deliverance Christ gives lays all human boasting in the dust. Man can claim no glory for the victories over temptation and sin. All the glory will go to God and will be proclaimed throughout all eternity:

"That no flesh should glory in His presence. But of Him you are in Christ Jesus, who became for us wisdom from God—and righteousness and sanctification and redemption—that, as it is written, 'He who glories, let him glory in the Lord'" (1 Cor. 1:29-31).

Bring us out of our spiritual darkness. Lord, arise in our midst and reveal the glory of Your character through us. Draw many in our community to the light of truth You have given us.

Personal Reflection and Discussion

1. Describe the path most Christians who have discovered the truth of "Christ in you, the hope of glory" have followed.

_____

_____

2. How will understanding and experiencing this truth change the Christian's life? Why is this truth important to understand and experience?

_____

_____

3. On a scale of 1-10, with 10 being high, how desirous are you to understand and experience the truth of abiding in Christ and Christ abiding in you? Explain your response.

_____

_____

Prayer Activity

- Call your prayer partner and discuss this devotional with him/her.
- Pray with your prayer partner:
    1. for God to continue to lead each of you with His Holy Spirit.
    2. for God to open your understanding of the biblical truth of abiding in Christ.
    3. for the individuals on your prayer list.

INCLUDE THE FOLLOWING BIBLE VERSE IN YOUR PRAYER:
"See, darkness covers the earth and thick darkness is over the peoples, but the Lord rises upon you and his glory appears over you. Nations will come to your light, and kings to the brightness of your dawn" (Isa. 60:2, 3, NIV).

Day 26

The Christian's Struggle

I titled today's devotional, "The Christian's Struggle," because the non-believer doesn't have the struggle that the Christian has. The unconverted man doesn't have the Spirit of God and is controlled only by his carnal mind. According to Paul, the carnal mind is "enmity against God; for it is not subject to the law of God, nor indeed can be" (Rom. 8:7). The non-Christian obeys for personal, selfish reasons, because of social pressure, etc. Or perhaps he was raised in a principled home and has a conscience that leads him to live a respectable life.

The Christian, on the other hand, obeys God because the Spirit of God has put the desire to obey in his heart:

"But God be thanked that though you were slaves of sin, yet you obeyed from the heart that form of doctrine to which you were delivered" (Rom. 6:17).

The born-again individual very much wants to carry out God's will in his life. Paul calls this delighting "in the law of God according to the inward man" (Rom. 7:22). Under the new covenant promise, the Holy Spirit begins writing God's law in his heart and mind (Heb. 8:8-10 and 2 Cor. 3:3).

However, the new believer discovers very quickly that there is another very strong desire in him—the desire for sin. Now that he has the Spirit of God, he is aware of his sinful desires, whereas before, many of those desires didn't really concern him. So the Christian discovers that there are now two natures residing in him: one that desires to follow sin, and the other that desires to obey God. Paul very clearly describes this intense conflict, experienced by every Christian, in Romans 7:14-25:

"For we know that the law is spiritual, but I am carnal, sold under sin. For what I am doing, I do not understand. For what I will to do, that I do not practice; but what I hate, that I do. If, then, I do what I will not to do, I agree with the law that it is good. But now, it is no longer I who do it, but sin that dwells in me. For I know that in me (that is, in my flesh) nothing good dwells; for to will is present with me, but how to perform what is good I do not find. For the good that I will to do, I do not do; but the evil I will not to do, that I practice. Now if I do what I will not to do, it is no longer I who do it, but sin that dwells in me. I find then a law, that evil is present with me, the one who wills to do good. For I delight in the law of God according to the inward man. But I see another law in my members, warring against the law of my mind, and bringing me into captivity to the law of sin which is in my members. O wretched man that I am! Who will deliver me from this body of death? I thank God—through Jesus Christ our Lord! So then, with the mind I myself serve the law of God, but with the flesh the law of sin."

Every Christian can identify with the struggle Paul describes. Christians often experience this struggle day after day, month after month, and year after year, and never obtain the victory they want to have over sin. Every Christian is well aware of the fact that there is a "law of sin" dwelling within them that is waging war against the God-given desire to obey His law. As Paul states, he delighted in God's law. He very much wanted to obey God in all things; however, he found that it was impossible for him to do so. His sinful nature constantly sought to make him a slave to the law of sin.

Recognizing the impossibility of obeying God because of the power of sin in his life, Paul cries out, "What a wretched man I am! Who will rescue me from this body of death?" He then declares that deliverance from the law of sin can happen "through Jesus Christ our Lord" (verses 24, 25, NIV).

In Romans 8:1-4, Paul gives the solution to this problem in the believer's life. The solution to the Christian's dilemma is to allow Christ Jesus, through the law of the Spirit of life, to set us free from the law of sin and death. Put another way, we must let Jesus live out His life in us through the baptism of the Holy Spirit. This is what Paul calls "walking in the Spirit." He further elaborates on this in his letter to the Galatians:

"I say then: Walk in the Spirit, and you shall not fulfill the lust of the flesh. For the flesh lusts against the Spirit, and the Spirit against the flesh; and these are contrary to one another, so that you do not do the things that you wish" (Gal. 5:16, 17).

Paul tells us that the righteous requirements of the law will be fulfilled "in us" when we have Jesus living in us through the baptism of the Holy Spirit:

"That the righteous requirement of the law might be fulfilled in us who do not walk according to the flesh but according to the Spirit" (Rom. 8:4).

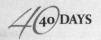

Personal Reflection and Discussion

1. What is the difference between the Christian's and the non-Christian's heartfelt attitude toward sin?

_____

_____

2. How does Paul describe the Christian's struggle with sin, and what is the solution?

_____

_____

3. What has been your experience with your personal struggle with sin?

_____

_____

Prayer Activity

- Call your prayer partner and discuss this devotional with him/her.
- Pray with your prayer partner:
    1. for God to continue to anoint each of you with His Holy Spirit.
    2. for God to bring revival into your life and His church.
    3. for God to lead you to experience genuine abiding in Christ for victory over sin.
    4. for the individuals on your prayer list.

INCLUDE THE FOLLOWING BIBLE VERSE IN YOUR PRAYER: "That the God of our Lord Jesus Christ, the Father of glory, may give to you the spirit of wisdom and revelation in the knowledge of Him, the eyes of your understanding being enlightened; that you may know what is the hope of His calling, what are the riches of the glory of His inheritance in the saints, and what is the exceeding greatness of His power toward us who believe, according to the working of His mighty power" (Eph. 1:17-19).

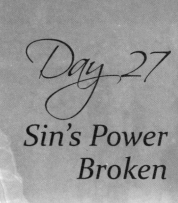

Day 27

Sin's Power Broken

There are many aspects to the good news of the gospel of Jesus Christ. One is that at the cross the power of the sinful nature was broken for all who accept Christ and believe:

"Knowing this, that our old man was crucified with Him, that the body of sin might be done away with, that we should no longer be slaves of sin" (Rom. 6:6). "Likewise you also, reckon yourselves to be dead indeed to sin, but alive to God in Christ Jesus our Lord" (verse 11).

When Jesus died on the cross, the power of the sinful nature in every believer's life was broken. This is a historical fact. However, it becomes a reality in the Christian's life only if he believes it.

This means that the unloving you, the unforgiving you, the angry you, the lustful you, the anxious you—the list could go on and on—died at the cross. That is wonderful news! It means that you do not have to be controlled by your unloving attitudes, your selfishness, anger, lustful thoughts and desires, etc. The power of these sinful desires, attitudes, and behaviors is broken.

The problem most Christians encounter when they read these Bible verses is that they conclude they should then be able to obey God with His help. For example, consider the Christian who has a struggle with anger. He reasons that if the power of his sinful anger was broken at the cross he now can stop being angry when something happens to cause him to become angry. He feels great relief, confident that now he will finally have the victory.

Soon something happens to cause him to feel anger. Perhaps someone cuts him off while driving, or someone says something unkind. Immediately anger arises. He puts forth efforts to subdue it, but he finds that it keeps lingering. He doesn't want these feelings, but seems helpless to get

rid of them. He begins questioning himself about why anger is still arising in his feelings. He concludes that he must not have asked God or received from God enough of His power to assist him in his efforts to overcome the anger. So he pleads with God to remove the anger, to give him the power needed, to give him the victory. Even so, he continues to experience the same pattern of being overcome by his besetting sins. More confusion and feelings of defeat set in. Again he questions his sincerity and has no peace in his walk with the Lord.

It is very true that the power of our sinful nature was broken at the cross. However, this does not mean that if we now believe this we can begin obeying God by putting forth efforts to do so. Remember, we have no ability in and of ourselves to obey God, even though the overwhelming influence of our sinful nature was broken at the cross. Simply knowing and believing that truth is not enough. No. There is only one way we will have the victory we long for. The victory over temptation and sin will take place in our lives only as we believe the truth of the crucifixion of our sinful nature and also allow Christ to give us His victory. We must understand that we will be victorious over sin and temptation only as we allow Him to live out His life of victory in us:

We will be victorious over sin and temptation only as we allow Him to live out His life of victory in us.

"For they being ignorant of God's righteousness, and seeking to establish their own righteousness, have not submitted to the righteousness of God. For Christ is the end of the law for righteousness to everyone who believes" (Rom. 10:3, 4).

"For to me, to live is Christ, and to die is gain" (Phil. 1:21).

Personal Reflection and Discussion

1. What happened to the power of the Christian's sinful nature at the cross? If one knows and believes this truth, does it mean they can now begin obeying God consistently? Why, or why not?

_____

_____

2. Have you ever asked God to remove a particular sin in your life, but your struggle with it continued? Have you felt like you were not a Christian because of recurring sins? How does God want you to deal with those feelings?

_____

_____

Prayer Activity

- Call your prayer partner and discuss this devotional with him/her.
- Pray with your prayer partner:
    1. for God to continue to fill each of you with His Holy Spirit.
    2. for God to help you let Jesus live out His life of victory in and through you.
    3. for the individuals on your prayer list.

INCLUDE THE FOLLOWING BIBLE VERSE IN YOUR PRAYER: "That [God] would grant you, according to the riches of His glory, to be strengthened with might through His Spirit in the inner man, that Christ may dwell in your hearts through faith; that you, being rooted and grounded in love, may be able to comprehend with all the saints what is the width and length and depth and height—to know the love of Christ which passes knowledge; that you may be filled with all the fullness of God" (Eph. 3:16-19).

Fill us with Your Spirit. Strengthen us by the power of Your Spirit so that we can stand against all the attacks of the enemy. Fill us with Your love and open our eyes to understand the love of Christ so we will reveal Christ's love to others by our words and actions.

Day 28

Christ Gives the Victory

Until the Christian comes to understand and experience what it means to let Christ give him His victory, he will not experience the consistently obedient life he desires. In today's devotional I will present how to let Christ live out His victorious life in you. When you come to understand and experience this truth, your Christian life will never again be the same. Instead of a life of sporadic obedience and broken promises to God, you will, in time, experience a life of victory through Christ over every temptation and sin that Satan brings your way.

Is such a consistently obedient life really possible? Can we truly have victory over every temptation and sin in our life? That is the kind of life God calls us to live in Romans 6:6 and 11-14.

Ellen White agrees:

"He who has not sufficient faith in Christ to believe that He can keep him from sinning, has not the faith that will give him an entrance into the kingdom of God" (Manuscript 161, 1897, p. 9).

So what is the answer to how we can live a consistently victorious Christian life? The answer is to let Jesus live out His life of victory in us, a truth taught throughout the Bible (Ps. 16:8; Isa. 26:3, 4; John 15:4, 5). These passages, and others, point to our dependence on Jesus and His guiding light in our lives.

Christ's mind was filled with pure, holy, virtuous thoughts. If we have asked Christ to live in us through the baptism of the Holy Spirit, if we believe He does, and if we believe He will manifest His love—His pure, holy, virtuous thoughts in our minds—He will do just that. It is a matter of faith—believing He will truly manifest Himself in our lives. Paul recognized this fact when he wrote Galatians 2:20 and Ephesians 3:16 and 17.

Believe Jesus will help you, and ask Him to manifest His virtue in you in relation to the temptation. Be specific. This happens as you daily receive the baptism of the Holy Spirit (John 14:16-18 and 1 John 3:24).

With Jesus living in you, you have His mind:

"For 'who has known the mind of the Lord that he may instruct Him?' But we have the mind of Christ" (1 Cor. 2:16).

We have His love, joy, peace, patience, gentleness, goodness, faith, meekness, temperance—all the fruit of the Spirit (Gal. 5:22, 23).

Through Jesus living in us via the baptism of the Holy Spirit, we have His likes and dislikes, His pure thoughts, His forgiveness—the list could go on and on. Every virtue of Christ is in you through Christ abiding in you.

How is the Christian to apply this truth? Simply put, the steps are these. When you become aware of a temptation to sin:

1. Choose to turn your mind immediately away from the temptation: "Finally, brethren, whatever things are true, whatever things are noble, whatever things are just, whatever things are pure, whatever things are lovely, whatever things are of good report, if there is any virtue and if there is anything praiseworthy—meditate on these things" (Phil. 4:8).

2. Believe that the power of your sinful nature's attraction to the temptation to control you is broken.

3. Believe Jesus is in you, and ask Him to manifest His virtue in you in relation to the temptation. Be specific.

4. Believe that He will manifest Himself in that manner, rest in that belief, and don't fight the temptation. When we fight the temptation we are actually focusing on it and trying to resist it in our own strength rather than looking to Jesus for the victory: "Therefore we also, since we are surrounded by so great a cloud of witnesses, let us lay aside every weight, and the sin which so easily ensnares us, and let us run with endurance the race that is set before us, looking unto Jesus, the author and finisher of our faith, who for the joy that was set before Him endured the cross, despising the shame, and has sat down at the right hand of the throne of God" (Heb. 12:1, 2).

5. Thank Him for the deliverance He has just given you.

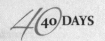

Personal Reflection and Discussion

1. What does the Bible teach about abiding in Jesus? Give Bible verses.

_____

_____

2. What is the benefit of having the Spirit dwell in you?

_____

_____

3. What are the steps to allow Jesus to give you victory over a temptation?

_____

_____

4. How do you plan to apply this teaching in your personal life?

_____

_____

Prayer Activity

- Call your prayer partner and discuss this devotional with him/her.
- Pray with your prayer partner:
    1. for God to continue to fill each of you with His Holy Spirit.
    2. for God to bring revival into your life and His church.
    3. for God to give you victory over your temptations through Jesus.
    4. for the individuals on your prayer list.

INCLUDE THE FOLLOWING BIBLE VERSE IN YOUR PRAYER:
"Now to Him who is able to do exceedingly abundantly above all that we ask or think, according to the power that works in us" (Eph. 3:20).

Open our understanding that we will never doubt Your power to deliver us from sin, to revive us individually and as a church, and to spread the gospel in our community. Help us to believe that the greatest power in this universe lives in us through Your Holy Spirit.

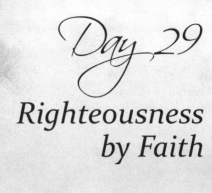

Day 29

Righteousness by Faith

Righteousness by faith is simply looking to Jesus to manifest His righteous life of victory in our life. God wants us to look to Christ for victory, not to ourselves:

"Therefore we also, since we are surrounded by so great a cloud of witnesses, let us lay aside every weight, and the sin which so easily ensnares us, and let us run with endurance the race that is set before us, looking unto Jesus, the author and finisher of our faith, who for the joy that was set before Him endured the cross, despising the shame, and has sat down at the right hand of the throne of God" (Heb. 12:1, 2).

This is true righteousness by faith and is God's will for every Christian. Oswald Chambers, a well-known Christian author, clearly presented this wonderful truth in the July 23 reading of his daily devotional, *My Utmost for His Highest:*

"But of Him you are in Christ Jesus, who became for us . . . sanctification" (1 Cor. 1:30).

"**The Life Side:** The most wonderful secret of living a holy life

> *The most wonderful secret of living a holy life does not lie in imitating Jesus, but in letting the perfect qualities of Jesus exhibit themselves in my human flesh.*

does not lie in imitating Jesus, but in letting the perfect qualities of Jesus exhibit themselves in my human flesh. Sanctification is 'Christ in you . . .' (Col. 1:27). It is His wonderful life that is imparted to me in sanctification—imparted by faith as a sovereign gift of God's grace. Am I willing for God to make sanctification as real in me as it is in His Word?

"Sanctification means the impartation of the holy qualities of Jesus Christ to me. It is the gift of His patience, love, holiness, faith, purity, and godliness that is exhibited in and through every sanctified soul. Sanctification is not

drawing from Jesus the power to be holy—it is drawing from Jesus the very holiness that was exhibited in Him, and that He now exhibits in me. Sanctification is an impartation, not an imitation. Imitation is something altogether different. The perfection of everything is in Jesus Christ, and the mystery of sanctification is that all the perfect qualities of Jesus are at my disposal. Consequently, I slowly but surely begin to live a life of inexpressible order, soundness, and holiness—'. . . kept by the power of God . . .' (1 Peter 1:5)."

Do you see the beauty of this truth? Our part is to look to Jesus in trusting faith, believing God's promise to manifest Christ and His righteousness in us. Our only part is to choose to let this happen and believe it will happen. When unrighteous desires and temptations come, we are not to fight against them. We are to turn to Christ and to ask Him to manifest His own righteousness (Heb. 12:1, 2). Then we are to wait in faith, believing He will do it.

Then when Jesus returns we will be able to stand in the very presence of Christ in all His glory and not be consumed. This is God's promise to His children, and it will be fulfilled as we learn to look to Jesus in faith for this marvelous manifestation of Himself in us:

"Now to Him who is able to keep you from stumbling, and to present you faultless before the presence of His glory with exceeding joy" (Jude 24).

Personal Reflection and Discussion

1. According to today's devotional study, what is God's will for every Christian?

_____

_____

2. Describe in your own words what Oswald Chambers wrote.

_____

_____

3. How do you plan to apply righteousness by faith to your personal life?

_____

_____

Prayer Activity

- Call your prayer partner and discuss this devotional with him/her.
- Pray with your prayer partner:
    1. for God to continue to anoint each of you with His Holy Spirit.
    2. for God to bring revival into your life and His church.
    3. for God to help you truly experience righteousness by faith in Christ alone.
    4. for the individuals on your prayer list.

INCLUDE THE FOLLOWING BIBLE VERSE IN YOUR PRAYER: "For I will pour water on him who is thirsty, and floods on the dry ground; I will pour My Spirit on your descendants, and My blessing on your offspring; they will spring up among the grass like willows by the watercourses" (Isa. 44:3, 4).

We are as dry ground spiritually—pour out Your Spirit on us and cause us to revive and grow into the fullness of Christ. May we faithfully live according to Your plans for our lives.

Day 30

God's Commandments and Abiding in Christ

Obedience to God's commandments and abiding in Christ go hand in hand. You cannot have one without the other. Jesus said: "If you keep My commandments, you will abide in My love, just as I have kept My Father's commandments and abide in His love" (John 15:10).

Jesus, the Holy Spirit, and God's law are inseparable. When we abide in Christ and He abides in us, the Ten Commandments will become an integral part of our life, because the Holy Spirit will be writing them on our heart:

"You are manifestly an epistle of Christ, ministered by us, written not with ink but by the Spirit of the living God, not on tablets of stone but on tablets of flesh, that is, of the heart" (2 Cor. 3:3).

In fact it was Jesus who before His incarnation gave Moses the Ten Commandments. The God who gave the commandments revealed Himself to Moses as the I AM (Ex. 3:14). Then, Jesus claimed to be the I AM of the Old Testament (John 8:58).

In Paul's letters we find many instructions concerning the attitudes and behaviors the Lord wants us to exhibit in our life. Paul gives very explicit instruction concerning behavior in Ephesians 4:22-32.

Why is so much space in the Bible given to inform us of the behavior God wants us to follow? The reason is that we need to know the attitudes and behaviors He wants us to have so that we can be aware of situations when we are tempted to behave wrongly. If we didn't know God's will in these areas, we wouldn't choose to let Christ manifest that aspect of His character in us. For example, if believers don't know it is wrong to hold onto anger and say something critical when someone wrongs them, they won't turn their thoughts away from the anger and critical spirit they begin to feel. They won't choose to let Christ manifest His "non-anger" and "noncritical spirit" in the situation because they are unaware that anger and a critical spirit are wrong. And so, they will not reflect Christ's character in that particular situation. They have not begun developing Christ's character within themselves in that area of their lives.

Also, the Ten Commandments are inseparably connected to love. Jesus made this very clear in His teachings (Matt. 19:16-19 and 22:35-40).

The apostle Paul taught that love and God's ten commandments refer to the same experience in one's life:

"Owe no one anything except to love one another, for he who loves another has fulfilled the law. For the commandments, 'You shall not commit adultery,' 'You shall not murder,' 'You shall not steal,' 'You shall not bear false witness,' 'You shall not covet,' and if there is any other commandment, are all summed up in this saying, namely, 'You shall love your neighbor as yourself.' Love does no harm to a neighbor; therefore love is the fulfillment of the law" (Rom. 13:8-10).

The first four commandments reveal how we love God, and the last six tell us how we are to love others. Hence, Christ abiding in us, the Ten Commandments, love, and intimately knowing Jesus are all closely related. You cannot have one without the others. John wrote of this close connection in his first letter:

"Now by this we know that we know Him, if we keep His commandments. He who says, 'I know Him,' and does not keep His commandments, is a liar, and the truth is not in him. But whoever keeps His word, truly the love of God is perfected in him. By this we know that we are in Him. He who says he abides in Him ought himself also to walk just as He walked" (1 John 2:3-6).

John clearly links our relationship with Jesus, His commandments, love, and abiding in Him together. He says that if we are abiding in Christ, we will be "walking," or living, as He lived. Why? Because we will be growing more and more like Jesus in love and character, our lives will be lives of obedience to God's Ten Commandments.

*Remove our lawbreaking tendencies from us—
give us a heart of obedience. Write your law in our
hearts that we may be faithful to Your Word.*

Personal Reflection and Discussion

1. How did Jesus connect abiding in Him and love with the Ten Commandments?

2. Where does God write the Ten Commandments today, and through what means?

3. How do you plan to apply the lesson of this devotional study to your life this week?

4. Do you desire to have a deeper experience of the Holy Spirit in your life and service for the Lord? Tell your prayer partner.

Prayer Activity

- Call your prayer partner and discuss this devotional with him/her.
- Pray with your prayer partner:
  1. for God to continue to fill each of you with His Holy Spirit.
  2. for God to bring revival into your life and His church.
  3. for God to write His ten-commandment law in your heart.
  4. for the individuals on your prayer list.

INCLUDE THE FOLLOWING BIBLE VERSE IN YOUR PRAYER:
"It is time for you to act, O Lord: your law is being broken"
(Ps. 119:126, NIV).

Abiding in Christ and Service

Service for the Lord can become a heavy burden at times, filled with anxiety and stress, before Christians come to understand and experience true abiding in Christ and His abiding in them. However, once the mystery of abiding in Christ is experienced, everything changes. Service for the Master is a joy, and the stress and burdens are relieved.

Ellen White wrote of the great peace Jesus had when He ministered on earth. Describing His response during the storm that threatened His disciples and Him, she wrote:

"When Jesus was awakened to meet the storm, He was in perfect peace. There was no trace of fear in word or look, for no fear was in His heart. But He rested not in the possession of almighty power. It was not as the 'Master of earth and sea and sky' that He reposed in quiet. That power He had laid down, and He says, 'I can of Mine own self do nothing.' John 5:30. He trusted in the Father's might. It was in

> **All fear, worry, and stress in service or life will be gone.**

faith—faith in God's love and care—that Jesus rested, and the power of that word which stilled the storm was the power of God" (*The Desire of Ages,* p. 336).

She goes on to challenge us to trust our Lord in the same manner:

"As Jesus rested by faith in the Father's care, so we are to rest in the care of our Saviour. If the disciples had trusted in Him, they would have been kept in peace. Their fear in the time of danger revealed their unbelief. In their efforts to save themselves, they forgot Jesus; and it was only when, in despair of self-dependence, they turned to Him that He could give them help.

"How often the disciples' experience is ours! When the tempests of temptation gather, and the fierce lightnings flash, and the waves sweep over us, we battle with the storm alone, forgetting that there is One who can help us. We trust in our own strength till our hope is lost, and we are ready to perish. Then we remember Jesus, and if we call upon Him to save us, we shall not cry in vain. . . . Whether on the land or on the sea, if we have the Saviour in our hearts, there is no need of fear. Living faith in the Redeemer will smooth the sea of life, and will deliver us from danger in the way that He knows to be best" (Ibid.).

When we are truly experiencing abiding in Christ and His abiding in us, His presence is a reality. Our resting in Him will then become real, not just a theory, and it will be consistent. All fear, worry, and stress in service or life will be gone. The burdens of ministry will be lifted, replaced with our resting in Jesus' presence. As Ellen White says, we must despair of self-dependency and turn to Christ.

When we are abiding in Christ, we will have the relationship with Him that He had with His Father, which enabled Him to rest in the assurance that the Father would speak and minister through Him.

"Do you not believe that I am in the Father, and the Father in Me? The words that I speak to you I do not speak on My own authority; but the Father who dwells in Me does the works" (John 14:10).

Cause us to trust in You, Lord, and not in earthly things, and then bless us abundantly.

Personal Reflection and Discussion

1. Was it unreasonable for the disciples to be fearful when they were in the boat in the storm? Why, or why not?

_____

_____

2. How do you usually react when trials, temptations, and difficulties come into your life?

_____

_____

3. How does God want you to react in difficult and trying situations?

_____

_____

4. How do you plan to apply the lesson of this devotional study to your life this week?

_____

_____

Prayer Activity

- Call your prayer partner and discuss this devotional with him/her.
- Pray with your prayer partner:
    1. for God to continue to fill each of you with His Holy Spirit.
    2. for God to bring revival into your life and His church.
    3. for God to remind you to look to Jesus and to trust Him when the next opportunity comes to serve Christ or a trial comes into your life.
    4. for the individuals on your prayer list.

INCLUDE THE FOLLOWING BIBLE VERSE IN YOUR PRAYER: "Oh, taste and see that the Lord is good; blessed is the man who trusts in Him!" (Ps. 34:8).

Day 32

The Sabbath Rest

The gospel is taught in the Creation story. In Genesis we read: "Thus the heavens and the earth, and all the host of them, were finished. And on the seventh day God ended His work which He had done, and He rested on the seventh day from all His work which He had done" (Gen. 2:1, 2).

Here we discover that God worked, then rested. The situation for Adam was just the opposite. First, he entered into God's rest, since the seventh-day Sabbath was his first full day of life. After entering God's rest on the seventh day, he then worked.

We begin experiencing God's redemptive work in our lives by resting in what God has already done for us.

The same sequence is true concerning our redemption. In Christ, God completed the work of redemption through His sinless life, death, and resurrection. We begin experiencing God's redemptive work in our lives by resting in what God has already done for us. We rest in the fact that Jesus died for our sins and has given to us eternal life as a free gift. We rest in the fact that we have Christ's righteousness covering us. We also rest in the fact that at the cross the power of our sinful nature was broken, and we are now free to serve God. Daily, we rest in the fact that Christ lives in us and will live out His life in and through us if we simply choose to let Him.

Once believers rest in these truths, they are able then to "work," or faithfully serve and obey God in life and ministry. This rest is necessary for them to faithfully serve God. By rest I mean that they accept by faith what God has done for their redemption, and trust implicitly in Christ.

In Hebrews 4 we find a similar description of the concept of rest in the story of Israel's failure to enter into God's rest during their wilderness sojourn:

"There remains therefore a rest for the people of God. For he who has entered His rest has himself also ceased from his works as God did from His. Let us therefore be diligent to enter that rest, lest anyone fall after the same example of disobedience" (Heb. 4:9-11).

God's Word is very clear about the concept of rest. When we enter into God's rest we cease our own efforts. We are told that it is important for us to seek to enter into this rest. Otherwise, we will fail in our obedience to God because of unbelief.

The only way to gain victory over temptation and sin is to rest in the fact that Jesus abides in us and to allow Him to live out His life in and through us. We must rest in that truth through belief and not hinder God's work of redemption in our life by trying to work or exert our own effort to obey. Our part is to believe and choose to let Christ live out His life in us. We are to rest in His completed work. This resting in Christ is the true meaning of the Sabbath rest God calls us to experience:

"Remember the Sabbath day, to keep it holy. Six days you shall labor and do all your work, but the seventh day is the Sabbath of the Lord your God. In it you shall do no work: you, nor your son, nor your daughter, nor your manservant, nor your maidservant, nor your cattle, nor your stranger who is within your gates. For in six days the Lord made the heavens and the earth, the sea, and all that is in them, and rested the seventh day. Therefore the Lord blessed the Sabbath day and hallowed it" (Ex. 20:8-11).

Our part is to choose and to believe. This requires 100 percent surrender to Christ 100 percent of the time.

Cause us to seek You and forsake our wicked ways and evil thoughts. Cause us to turn to You with our whole heart. Have mercy on us and pardon us. Help us to experience true Sabbath rest as You originally intended.

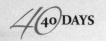

Personal Reflection and Discussion

1. How is the gospel taught in the creation account?

_____

_____

2. What truths about Jesus are Christians to rest in?

_____

_____

3. How is resting in Jesus connected with an obedient Christian life?

_____

_____

4. What is the true meaning of Sabbath rest?

_____

_____

Prayer Activity

● **Call your prayer partner and discuss this devotional with him/her.**
● **Pray with your prayer partner:**
   1. **for God to continue to fill each of you with His Holy Spirit.**
   2. **for God to bring revival into your life and His church.**
   3. **for God to lead you to enter into the true meaning of Sabbath rest.**
   4. **for the individuals on your prayer list.**

INCLUDE THE FOLLOWING BIBLE VERSE IN YOUR PRAYER:
"Seek the Lord while he may be found; call on him while he is near. Let the wicked forsake his way and the evil man his thoughts. Let him turn to the Lord, and he will have mercy on him, and to our God, for he will freely pardon" (Isa. 55:6, 7, NIV).

Day 33

Something Missing

The baptism of the Holy Spirit is an experience necessary for Christians if they are to become truly like Jesus in life and ministry. As a result of this intimate connection with Jesus, we will begin to experience our greatest victories over sin and will develop the most meaningful relationship possible with our Savior.

The relationship between the baptism of the Holy Spirit and genuine Christian fellowship is also essential for the Christian to understand and experience. Even though we may receive the baptism of the Holy Spirit, we will not grow spiritually as God intends without a meaningful, mutually dependent fellowship with other Spirit-filled believers. To become Spirit-filled, and remain somewhat isolated and independent of other Spirit-filled Christians, will not only hinder our spiritual growth but may lead to the loss of the fullness of the Spirit's presence in our life.

The average fellowship consists of warm greetings before and after church.

Bible-focused denominations, including Seventh-day Adventists, tend to be very intellectual in their religion. We know many vital truths of the Bible. Our evangelistic efforts focus on those truths that set us apart from other denominations. Hence, many who choose to become church members do so because of those truths.

One fact that has often troubled me is the general weakness of Seventh-day Adventists in the area of Christian fellowship. We are a rather independent group of believers. One has to have somewhat of an independent spirit to become a Seventh-day Adventist in the first place, for choosing to keep the seventh-day Sabbath sets us apart from the majority of other Christians.

I have often read the description of the believers following Pentecost:

"And they continued steadfastly in the apostles' doctrine and fellowship, in the breaking of bread, and in prayers" (Acts 2:42).

I knew we were "right on," as a church, when it came to doctrine. However, when it came to fellowship we didn't fare so well. I have observed that most Adventists are hard workers who provide for their families and do their best to attend the Sabbath morning worship service. Most church services are somewhat formal, with little or no time for interaction between believers. Hence, the average fellowship consists of warm greetings before and after church. Then most make their way home to return the next Sabbath. Many of our churches have a midweek prayer meeting, which usually consists of a biblical presentation by the pastor and a season of prayer. However, most of our church members feel they are too busy or too tired to attend this midweek service.

I have often felt that as Seventh-day Adventist Christians, fellowship should play a more important role than it does. The next seven devotionals will show why Spirit-filled Christians must enter into close fellowship with others who are Spirit-filled if they want to grow into the fullness of Christ and be ready for His return.

Have compassion on us and deliver us from our sinfulness. Restore us to spiritual strength, and help us to find like-minded Christians to fellowship with and prepare for Your return.

Personal Reflection and Discussion

1. What are the characteristics of the early Christian church, as listed in Acts 2:42?

_____

_____

2. Reflect on how much genuine Christian fellowship you are now having, or have had in the past.

_____

_____

3. Why do you think Christian fellowship is necessary to be ready for Christ's second coming? What benefit does it provide the believer?

_____

_____

4. Why do you think Christian fellowship is necessary in order to be ready for Christ's second coming?

_____

_____

Prayer Activity

- Call your prayer partner and discuss this devotional with him/her.
- Pray with your prayer partner:
    1. for God to continue to fill each of you with His Holy Spirit.
    2. for God to bring revival into your life and His church.
    3. for God to open your understanding as to why Christian fellowship is important.
    4. for the individuals on your prayer list.

INCLUDE THE FOLLOWING BIBLE VERSE IN YOUR PRAYER:
"'Though the mountains be shaken and the hills be removed, yet my unfailing love for you will not be shaken nor my covenant of peace be removed,' says the Lord, who has compassion on you" (Isa. 54:10, NIV).

Day 34

The Early Church and Fellowship

I personally believe the Lord is moving upon His people to look more closely at what the New Testament church was like. Seventh-day Adventists have viewed themselves as God's remnant for many years. We have sought to hold true to the teachings of God's Word, as did the New Testament church. I believe that now the Lord is calling us not only to continue "steadfastly in the apostles' doctrine," but to continue steadfastly in "fellowship, in the breaking of bread, and in prayers (Acts 2:42). God is calling His children to be His remnant people just like the New Testament early church, not only in doctrine but in fellowship, as well. Fellowship is an important aspect to being God's remnant people. With this in mind, let's take a closer look at what God's early church was like.

The book of Acts tells us that the early Christians met both in the Temple and from house to house:

"So continuing daily with one accord in the temple, and breaking bread from house to house, they ate their food with gladness and simplicity of heart" (verse 46).

As the Christians became unwelcome in the Jewish temples, their homes became their primary place of worship and fellowship. The homes of the believers were the places where they met for praise, fellowship, and teaching. Many verses mention the homes in the New Testament where the Christians met (Acts 20:20; Rom. 16:5; 1 Cor. 1:16; 1 Cor. 16:19; Col. 4:15). Following are a few select verses that illustrate their fellowship together:

"And when they had entered, they went up into the upper room where they were staying: Peter, James, John, and Andrew; Philip and Thomas; Bartholomew and Matthew; James the son of Alphaeus and Simon the Zealot; and Judas the son of James" (Acts 1:13).

"Now a certain woman named Lydia heard us. She was a seller of purple from the city of Thyatira, who worshiped God. The Lord opened her heart to heed the things spoken by Paul. And when she and her household were baptized, she begged us, saying, 'If you have judged me to be faithful to the Lord, come to my house and stay.' And she constrained us" (Acts 16:14, 15).

"But the Jews who were not persuaded, becoming envious, took some of the evil men from the marketplace, and gathering a mob, set all the city in an uproar and attacked the house of Jason, and sought to bring them out to the people. But when they did not find them, they dragged Jason and some brethren to the rulers of the city, crying out, 'These who have turned the world upside down have come here too. Jason has harbored them, and these are all acting contrary to the decrees of Caesar, saying there is another king—Jesus.' And they troubled the crowd and the rulers of the city when they heard these things. So when they had taken security from Jason and the rest, they let them go" (Acts 17:5-9).

The apostles certainly understood the importance of a small home fellowship. For three and one half years they had worshipped and fellowshipped with Jesus in this manner. We can understand how natural it was for the apostles to continue this type of small group fellowship as hundreds and thousands of individuals accepted Christ. The home fellowship style of church would make it much easier to assimilate and organize the large numbers joining the church even on a daily basis:

"Praising God and having favor with all the people. And the Lord added to the church daily those who were being saved" (Acts 2:47).

These small fellowship groups served the growth of the church well. It is estimated that by the third century six million Christians lived in the Roman Empire. These small fellowship groups were conducive to growth. New members were assimilated quickly and thoroughly. It would also be evident that these groups were not just to nurture but were evangelistic in nature. The home groups enabled the church to grow even in times of severe persecution. Also, as the numbers of a home church grew, participants would be forced to divide and form a new group in another home.

The close, intimate fellowship that results from the smaller group creates a very close bond between members of the group. Mutual encouragement more readily takes place. It is in this kind of setting that fellow believers receive strength from one another. Humankind is created to stand stronger when united with others than when alone. Christians today need the strength that comes from the close, intimate fellowship the early church experienced. As God said in the beginning, "it is not good for the man to be alone" (Gen. 2:18, NIV). It is not good for the Christian to try to withstand the forces of Satan and the world alone.

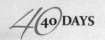

Personal Reflection and Discussion

1. Where did the early Christians meet for fellowship, and why?

_____

_____

2. What are the benefits of home fellowship groups?

_____

_____

3. Do you think there will be a time when home fellowship will become necessary? Why, or why not?

_____

_____

4. Would you like to be a part of a Spirit-filled home fellowship group? If yes, how can you become part of one?

_____

_____

Prayer Activity

- Call your prayer partner and discuss this devotional with him/her.
- Pray with your prayer partner:
    1. for God to continue to fill each of you with His Holy Spirit.
    2. for God to bring revival into your life and His church.
    3. for God to lead you to become part of a fellowship group.
    4. for the individuals on your prayer list.

INCLUDE THE FOLLOWING BIBLE VERSE IN YOUR PRAYER: "I have set watchmen on your walls, O Jerusalem, who shall never hold their peace day or night. You who make mention of the Lord, do not keep silent, and give Him no rest till He establishes and till He makes Jerusalem a praise in the earth" (Isa. 62:6, 7).

Spirit Baptism and Fellowship Groups

The baptism of the Holy Spirit and fellowship groups go hand in hand. Both are necessary for the Christian to grow into the fullness of Christ. The baptism of the Holy Spirit is essential for the core members of a fellowship group in order for the group to function as God intends. We see this clearly illustrated in the experience of Christ and the disciples. The 12 disciples were in a very close personal, group relationship with Christ and one another for three and a half years. Yet we find them bickering among themselves on the way to the Passover supper just before Christ was to be taken by the mob and ultimately crucified:

"But there was also rivalry among them, as to which of them should be considered the greatest" (Luke 22:24).

They had not yet attained the level of loving, committed fellowship with God or each other during those years. Simply being a part of a fellowship group, of which Christ was the leader, was not enough to bring about the changes necessary for them to grow up into the fullness of Christ. Later, we find that they were changed dramatically. What made the difference? Their receiving the baptism of the Holy Spirit on the day of Pentecost made the difference. From that day forward they, and all others who were present, entered into the genuine Christian fellowship that God desires every believer to experience:

"And they continued steadfastly in the apostles' doctrine and fellowship, in the breaking of bread, and in prayers" (Acts 2:42). "So continuing daily with one accord in the temple, and breaking bread from house to house, they ate their food with gladness and simplicity of heart, praising God and having favor with all the people. And the Lord added to the church daily those who were being saved" (verses 46, 47).

The early church's fellowship way of doing church cannot happen during the traditional Sabbath morning worship service because of the

interrelational dynamics required between Spirit-filled believers. The only way this kind of fellowship experience can happen is in small Christian fellowship groups. The traditional Sabbath worship service is important. The point is, that alone is not enough.

The importance of Spirit-filled believers fellowshipping together in small groups is demonstrated by two illustrations. Paul gives us one illustration of the necessity of a continued living connection between believers in his first letter to the Corinthians, chapter 12. He uses the analogy of the human body to describe the church and its members. He points out how necessary it is for each body part to minister to the body. Spirit-filled believers need one another. They are to minister to one another just as your heart, right hand, eyes, etc., minister to the other parts of your body. From this analogy it is evident that it is necessary for each body part to remain in close, living connection with the other body parts. It is the home fellowship groups that enable the Spirit-baptized believer to keep a close, living connection with the body of Christ, which enables members of the body to minister to one another:

"But the manifestation of the Spirit is given to each one for the profit of all: for to one is given the word of wisdom through the Spirit, to another the word of knowledge through the same Spirit, to another faith by the same Spirit, to another gifts of healings by the same Spirit, to another the working of miracles, to another prophecy, to another discerning of spirits, to another different kinds of tongues, to another the interpretation of tongues. But one and the same Spirit works all these things, distributing to each one individually as He wills. For as the body is one and has many members, but all the members of that one body, being many, are one body, so also is Christ" (1 Cor. 12:7-12).

Paul also speaks about the body of Christ in Ephesians 4:11-16.

Another illustration of the importance of home fellowship groups can be seen around any campfire. Think for a moment of a time when you were sitting around a campfire and watching the embers burn. In order to keep the fire going it was important that you kept the embers close together and occasionally put on new wood. If a burning ember became separated from the other burning embers it would soon lose its fire and go out. This clearly illustrates the importance of close Christian fellowship. In order for the Spirit-baptized believer to keep the "fire" from going out in his life, he needs not only to continually ask God for the Spirit's infilling (Eph. 5:18), but he must also continually keep in fellowship with other Spirit-filled believers.

Personal Reflection and Discussion

1. What is the relationship between the baptism of the Holy Spirit and Christian fellowship groups?

_____

_____

2. Was the disciples' association with Jesus for three-and-a-half years enough to prepare them for the close fellowship Jesus wanted them to have? Why, or why not?

_____

_____

3. Do you feel close Christian fellowship is important for your spiritual life? Why?

_____

_____

Prayer Activity

- Call your prayer partner and discuss this devotional with him/her.
- Pray with your prayer partner:
   1. for God to continue to fill each of you with His Holy Spirit.
   2. for God to bring revival into your life and His church.
   3. for God to bless your efforts to become part of a fellowship group.
   4. for the individuals on your prayer list.

INCLUDE THE FOLLOWING BIBLE VERSE IN YOUR PRAYER:
"My soul is weary with sorrow; strengthen me according to your word" (Ps. 119:28, NIV).

My sinful condition has weakened me. Turn me from my sin, and strengthen me spiritually as You have promised. Make me an active part of your body of believers.

Day 36

The Church

The Greek word used in the New Testament for church is *ekklesia,* which means "called-out ones." When men and women respond to the Holy Spirit's conviction to accept Christ as their Savior, they become part of ekklesia, the called-out ones.

When we study the New Testament we discover that there are two very important aspects of church. Those who are called out are called to believe the teachings of the Bible. Paul describes the church with these words:

"But if I am delayed, I write so that you may know how you ought to conduct yourself in the house of God, which is the church of the living God, the pillar and ground of the truth" (1 Tim. 3:15).

Paul calls the church the "pillar and ground of the truth." Those called out are to believe, live, and teach the truths of God's Word.

There is another important aspect of church revealed in John's first letter:

"That which we have seen and heard we declare to you, that you also may have fellowship with us; and truly our fellowship is with the Father and with His Son Jesus Christ" (1 John 1:3).

Fellowship means sharing one another's hopes, dreams, struggles, and pains. It means allowing God to use us to minister to one another.

This second vital aspect of church is what the New Testament calls "fellowship." In the simplest sense, fellowship is certainly not a new concept. In fact, in one sense we fellowship when we worship at church on Sabbath or when we attend a church social together. However, the New Testament concept of fellowship is much broader than most Christians realize.

The Greek word translated fellowship is *koinonia.* The noun form of this term means to share in, participate in, or to be actively involved in. The verb form means to communicate, distribute, and impart. Hence, to *koinonia* together means much more than simply sitting together in the sanctuary for Sabbath worship or playing games together at a social. The New Testament meaning of fellowship goes much deeper. In essence, it means ministering to one another. It is not simply knowing one another's names, knowing where we live, and warmly greeting one another at church Sabbath morning. It means sharing one another's hopes, dreams, struggles, and pains. It means allowing God to use us to minister to one another. According to the New Testament, a church fellowship is an assembly of individuals, called out of the world by God to become a community, with common biblical beliefs and who actively communicate, distribute, impart, and minister to one another.

If Christians are not in that kind of relationship with one another, they are falling far short of God's plan for His church. We may be keeping the Sabbath and going to church, but if we are not in genuine *koinonia* Christian fellowship, we are not actually experiencing God's definition of church to the fullest extent.

Cause us to fear and reverence You with all our hearts. Deliver us from the things that keep us from having what we need spiritually. Help us to find true fellowship with other believers.

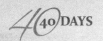

Personal Reflection and Discussion

1. What does the word *church* mean in the New Testament?

_____

_____

2. What are two aspects of the Christian church in the New Testament?

_____

_____

3. What does it mean to be in *koinonia* fellowship with one another?

_____

_____

4. Are you involved in *koinonia* fellowship with any Christians?
If yes, what has been your experience with this kind of fellowship?
If no, would you like to be in this kind of fellowship?

_____

_____

Prayer Activity

- Call your prayer partner and discuss this devotional with him/her.
- Pray with your prayer partner:
    1. for God to continue to baptize each of you with His Holy Spirit.
    2. for God to bring revival into your life and His church.
    3. for God to bless your efforts to become part of a koinonia fellowship group, or to bless your fellowship group if you are in one.
    4. or the individuals on your prayer list.

INCLUDE THE FOLLOWING BIBLE VERSE IN YOUR PRAYER:
"Oh, fear the Lord, you His saints! There is no want to those who fear Him" (Ps. 34:9).

Day 37

The Family of God

Sin broke apart the family of God. The plan of redemption was established to restore this family. Paul addresses those who have responded to God's call in their lives in the following way:

"Now, therefore, you are no longer strangers and foreigners, but fellow citizens with the saints and members of the household of God" (Eph. 2:19).

The Greek word translated "household" is oikeios. When we become a believer in Jesus Christ we become a member of God's household. We become a member of His family.

Traditionally, we tend to think of church in a larger sense, the corporate or congregational aspect. We do not tend to think of church in terms of a smaller family. However, the early church from the biblical and historical perspective was made up of small home fellowships. These fellowship groups functioned as family.

When Paul describes his own feelings toward the Thessalonica family of God, he expresses the relationship that is to be experienced in the family of God:

> *In a loving family the members are there to encourage one another with words and actions.*

"We loved you so much that we were delighted to share with you not only the gospel of God but our lives as well, because you had become so dear to us" (1 Thess. 2:8, NIV).

These kinds of endearing relationships cannot happen in the larger congregational setting. If our church activities consist primarily of coming to church on Sabbath morning, greeting our friends, and then returning home, we cannot possibly achieve this level of family relationship.

For example, what if you heard about a family that remained separated

from one another during the week and then came together once a week for an hour or two, briefly greeted one another, then sat in rows, and heard someone give a lecture. Afterward, they went their separate ways until seven days later when they associated "together" by again greeting one another, sitting in rows, and listening to another lecture. What would you think about that family's togetherness? I think you would question if they were really a family. Most would certainly conclude that their style of family togetherness had much room for improvement. Amazingly and yet sadly, most Christians seek to be a church family using this pattern of family.

In a healthy family the members know each other intimately. They know one another's fears, hopes, dreams, frustrations, and struggles. In a loving, caring family the members are there to encourage one another with words and actions.

The family of God is to function in the same way. However, God's family has one significant advantage over the average family in the world. God's family experiences the fruit and gifts of the Spirit functioning in their midst. God Himself is the One ministering to the family members. He does this through each member of the family as they continue to receive the baptism of the Holy Spirit. The intimate relationship with God this daily baptism brings allows Christ to live in and minister through each believer, but this dynamic of family can take place only in the smaller fellowship group setting.

Personal Reflection and Discussion

1. What kind of relationship did God originally plan for His children?
What did sin do to God's plan?

_____

_____

2. What does the plan of redemption do for God's broken family?

_____

_____

3. What kind of relationships does God intend His church members
to have with one another?

_____

_____

4. What setting is most conducive for this to happen?

_____

_____

Prayer Activity

● Call your prayer partner and discuss this devotional with him/her.
● Pray with your prayer partner:
  1. for God to continue to baptize each of you with His Holy Spirit.
  2. for God to bring revival into your life and His church.
  3. for God to lead you into the kind of church family experience
     He desires for you.
  4. for the individuals on your prayer list.

INCLUDE THE FOLLOWING BIBLE VERSE IN YOUR PRAYER:
"Many are the afflictions of the righteous, but the Lord delivers him
out of them all" (Ps. 34:19).

Day 38

The Fruit of the Spirit and Fellowship

Two essential elements of effective Christian fellowship groups are the fruit and gifts of the Spirit manifested in the lives of the participants. There is only one way these can be present: the participants must be Spirit-filled.

In today's devotional we will consider the role the fruit of the Spirit play in fellowship. If the fruit of the Spirit are not present and maturing in the participants' lives, they will not receive the full benefit of the fellowship group. Neither will they have the character necessary to minister to their fellow participants. The fruit of the Spirit are listed in Paul's letter to the Galatians:

"But the fruit of the Spirit is love, joy, peace, longsuffering, kindness, goodness, faithfulness, gentleness, self-control. Against such there is no law" (Gal. 5:22, 23).

The first fruit is love. The Greek word here is agape love, the highest form of love. It is the kind of love with which God loves us, doing what is best for the one loved. Jesus described this kind of love in Matthew 5:44:

"But I say to you, love your enemies, bless those who curse you, do good to those who hate you, and pray for those who spitefully use you and persecute you."

Paul described agape love in 1 Corinthians 13:4-7:

"Love suffers long and is kind; love does not envy; love does not parade itself, is not puffed up; does not behave rudely, does not seek its own, is not provoked, thinks no evil; does not rejoice in iniquity, but rejoices in the truth; bears all things, believes all things, hopes all things, endures all things."

This fruit of love will allow the participant of a fellowship group to manifest understanding and sensitivity to others in the group. Their example will tend to quiet any harsh tones or attitudes in others. Also, they will not have a judgmental attitude when a participant shares with the group their personal struggles. Rather, the fruit of love will cause them to feel empathy and compassion. They will reach out with healing, encouraging, redemptive words to the one hurting.

Every fruit that follows in Paul's list plays a similarly significant role in maintaining the kind of atmosphere that is necessary for the Christian fellowship group to function as God intends.

These qualities, which comprise the fruit of the Spirit, are impossible to achieve apart from the infilling of the Spirit. Spirit-filled Christians are necessary if the fellowship group is to fulfill its purpose of providing an atmosphere in which all participants can grow into the fullness of Christ:

"And He Himself gave some to be apostles, some prophets, some evangelists, and some pastors and teachers, for the equipping of the saints for the work of ministry, for the edifying of the body of Christ, till we all come to the unity of the faith and of the knowledge of the Son of God, to a perfect man, to the measure of the stature of the fullness of Christ; that we should no longer be children, tossed to and fro and carried about with every wind of doctrine, by the trickery of men, in the cunning craftiness by which they lie in wait to deceive, but, speaking the truth in love, may grow up in all things into Him who is the head—Christ—from whom the whole body, joined and knit together by what every joint supplies, according to the effective working by which every part does its share, causes growth of the body for the edifying of itself in love" (Eph. 4:11-16).

It is through people that God loves us. So it will be through Spirit-filled Christians that God will reveal His love to all who come to the fellowship, whether they are Christian or non-Christian.

The fruit of the Spirit, which are manifest in the life of the believer only by the baptism of the Holy Spirit, must be present in the lives of the core members of the fellowship group. These fruit bring the character of Christ into the group. It is through people that God loves us. So it will be through Spirit-filled Christians that God will reveal His love to all who come to the fellowship, whether they are Christian or non-Christian.

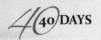

Personal Reflection and Discussion

1. What must each fellowship participant have in order for the fruit of the Spirit to be present?

_____

2. List the fruit of the Spirit and describe how each one is a blessing to those in the fellowship group.

_____
_____
_____
_____
_____
_____
_____

3. How do you plan to become a part of this kind of fellowship group?

_____

Prayer Activity

- Call your prayer partner and discuss this devotional with him/her.
- Pray with your prayer partner:
    1. for God to continue to fill each of you with His Holy Spirit.
    2. for God to manifest the fruit of the Spirit in your life and to lead you to a Spirit-filled fellowship group.
    3. for the individuals on your prayer list.

INCLUDE THE FOLLOWING BIBLE VERSE IN YOUR PRAYER:
"Bear one another's burdens and so fulfill the law of Christ"
(Gal. 6:2).

*Glorify Your name in our fellowship together,
in this congregation and in the world
as we bear one another's burdens.*

Day 39

The Gifts of the Spirit and Fellowship

Another essential ingredient for a fellowship group to be successful is the functioning of the gifts of the Spirit in the group. Since spiritual gifts are manifested through Spirit-filled believers, it is essential that the participants be baptized in the Holy Spirit.

Several chapters in the New Testament discuss spiritual gifts. The most prominent Scriptures concerning spiritual gifts are found in Paul's letters:

"For as we have many members in one body, but all the members do not have the same function, so we, being many, are one body in Christ, and individually members of one another. Having then gifts differing according to the grace that is given to us, let us use them: if prophecy, let us prophesy in proportion to our faith; or ministry, let us use it in our ministering; he who teaches, in teaching; he who exhorts, in exhortation; he who gives, with liberality; he who leads, with diligence; he who shows mercy, with cheerfulness" (Rom. 12:4-8).

"But the manifestation of the Spirit is given to each one for the profit of all: for to one is given the word of wisdom through the Spirit, to another the word of knowledge through the same Spirit, to another faith by the same Spirit, to another gifts of healings by the same Spirit, to another the working of miracles, to another prophecy, to another discerning of spirits, to another different kinds of tongues, to another the interpretation of tongues. But one and the same Spirit works all these things, distributing to each one individually as He wills. For as the body is one and has many members, but all the members of that one body, being many, are one body, so also is Christ" (1 Cor. 12:7-12).

"But to each one of us grace was given according to the measure of Christ's gift. Therefore He says: 'When He ascended on high, He led captivity captive, and gave gifts to men.' . . . And He Himself gave some to be apostles, some prophets, some evangelists, and some pastors and teachers" (Eph. 4:7-11).

These gifts serve a most important role in the spiritual growth of the individual believer and the church. Paul uses the analogy of the human body and lists various body parts, pointing out the importance each part plays in the functioning of the whole body. The conclusion is clear. It is necessary that every body part function effectively in order for the body as a whole to be healthy and effective in fulfilling its mission (1 Cor. 12:14-22).

Paul states that "the members should have the same care for one another" (verse 25). When functioning in the church body, the gifts prove a great blessing to each member of the body of Christ.

It should be very clear from Paul's description that the gifts of the Spirit are necessary if the individual Christian and church are to grow. Paul's statement that members should have the "same care for one another" is a clear reference to genuine Christian fellowship. In order to experience a deep empathy for our fellow members we must truly know them. We must be free to share our deepest needs, struggles, hopes, and dreams if we are to minister to one another. Paul was referring to the importance of ministering to one another when he wrote:

"Bear one another's burdens, and so fulfill the law of Christ" (Gal. 6:2).

This kind of fellowship cannot happen by doing church in the traditional way. If our only connection with the members of our church is meeting them on Sabbath morning and giving them a warm greeting, it will be impossible for biblical fellowship to happen.

The gifts of the Spirit will function in a very practical manner in blessing those in fellowship. For example, the gift of teacher in the New Testament is one who instructs in God's Word. It is readily understood how vital it is to have this gift in a fellowship group. The gift of teaching that fits into this purpose will be a great blessing to all who attend. The lessons will be generally short ones from Scripture rather than a long teaching session. The emphasis will be placed on the practical application of Scripture to the individual issues that arise in the group setting.

Another example is the gift of exhortation. When this gift is present, God will use it to speak words of encouragement, comfort, and hope, especially to group participants who are hurting and dealing with some serious issue in their lives. The manifestation of this gift brings practical, uplifting biblical counsel to the group members. Such spiritual gifts being manifested in a Christian fellowship group will enable the Spirit to minister to all participants.

Personal Reflection and Discussion

1. What must each fellowship participant have so that the gifts of the Spirit are present?

_____

2. List several gifts of the Spirit and describe how each one will be used by God to minister to those in the fellowship group.

_____
_____
_____
_____
_____
_____
_____
_____

3. Have you seen God manifest spiritual gifts through you to minister to others? If yes, which gifts?

_____
_____

Prayer Activity

- Call your prayer partner and discuss this devotional with him/her.
- Pray with your prayer partner:
    1. for God to continue to fill each of you with His Holy Spirit.
    2. for God to bring revival into your life and His church.
    3. for God to use you to minister to others through the gifts of the Spirit.
    4. for the individuals on your prayer list.

INCLUDE THE FOLLOWING BIBLE VERSE IN YOUR PRAYER:
"For in fact the body is not one member but many. . . . But now God has set the members, each one of them, in the body just as He pleased" (1 Cor. 12:14, 18).

Day 40

Fellowship Groups and Church Growth

The fellowship of believers will play an important role in their spiritual, emotional, and even physical restoration that God wants each one of us to experience.

Growth should—and must—be the goal of every Christian fellowship group. If the group is not growing, it is not functioning in the manner God intends. Remember, the baptism of the Holy Spirit is given for both our personal spiritual growth and for the spreading of the gospel:

"But you shall receive power when the Holy Spirit has come upon you; and you shall be witnesses to Me in Jerusalem, and in all Judea and Samaria, and to the end of the earth" (Acts 1:8).

Hence, nonbelievers, or individuals who are not church members, should be present.

It is essential for our own personal spiritual growth to be involved in winning others to Christ. We must personally heed God's command to be "fruitful and multiply" (Gen. 1:28). God could have used angels for the work of soul winning; however, He did not. Why? He knows the importance of each of us being personally involved in reaching others for Christ. Ellen White makes a significant statement concerning this:

"If you will go to work as Christ designs that His disciples shall, and win souls for Him, you will feel the need of a deeper experience and a greater knowledge in divine things, and will hunger and thirst after righteousness. You will plead with God, and your faith will be strengthened, and your soul will drink deeper drafts at the well of salvation. Encountering opposition and trials will drive you to the Bible and prayer. You will grow in grace and the knowledge of Christ, and will develop a rich experience" (*Steps to Christ,* p. 80).

The support the fellowship group gives will play a significant role in our efforts to reach out to others. The members of the group will join in prayer for those we are reaching out to. The counsel of those more experienced in soul winning will be a great benefit to us. The spiritual fathers and mothers in the group will be used by God to assist the less experienced in leading others to Christ.

The fellowship group will provide a marvelous environment for those seeking God, for they will find loving, caring individuals who will accept them as they are. Seekers will find themselves in an environment in which God's Spirit can work in a powerful way for their conversion to Christ. We read in the book of Acts that as the early Christians continued to fellowship together the church grew:

"So continuing daily with one accord in the temple, and breaking bread from house to house, they ate their food with gladness and simplicity of heart, praising God and having favor with all the people. And the Lord added to the church daily those who were being saved" (Acts 2:46, 47).

God will minister to both the believers and nonbelievers who are present in the fellowship group. He will do this by means of the fruits and gifts of the Spirit. The small fellowship group setting completely changes the traditional impersonal dynamic of evangelism when individuals attend an evangelistic meeting in response to a mailed advertisement. The very essence of the fellowship group is close, intimate, interpersonal relationships. When nonbelievers come to experience Christianity and new biblical truths in the setting of this fellowship, they do so in the context of a close interpersonal relationship with the members of the group. They are placed in a redemptive environment that is conducive to their personal spiritual growth.

Lead us to pray for the early rain baptism of the Holy Spirit in our lives and for the latter rain outpouring of Your Holy Spirit. Manifest the gifts of Your Spirit through us and use us to glorify Your name. Reveal Your power in our midst and in our community that many will come to know You as their God and Savior.

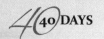
Personal Reflection and Discussion

1. What are two purposes of genuine Christian fellowship groups?

_____

_____

2. List suggestions on how a fellowship group can become effective in reaching others outside the group for Christ?

_____

_____

_____

_____

_____

_____

3. How do you plan to become part of a growing fellowship group and be used by God to share Christ with others?

_____

_____

Prayer Activity

- Call your prayer partner and discuss this devotional with him/her.
- Pray with your prayer partner:
    1. for God to continue to pour out His Holy Spirit on each of you.
    2. for God to bring revival into your life and His church.
    3. for God to lead you to become part of a growing fellowship group and be used by Him to bring others to Christ.
    4. for the individuals on your prayer list.

INCLUDE THE FOLLOWING BIBLE VERSE IN YOUR PRAYER:
"I will pour out My Spirit on all flesh; your sons and your daughters shall prophesy, your old men shall dream dreams, your young men shall see visions" (Joel 2:28).

After the 40 Days of Prayer and Devotional Studies. . .

Now that you have completed the 40 days of prayer and devotional studies, you probably don't want the experience you are having with the Lord and the fellowship you are enjoying to fade away. So, what should you do next?

One possibility is that you begin studying in greater detail the subjects presented in this devotional. Each section has been based on one of five books I have written. The titles of the books in the order of the devotional sections are:

- *The Baptism of the Holy Spirit*
- *Spirit Baptism and Prayer*
- *Spirit Baptism and Evangelism*
- *Spirit Baptism and Abiding in Christ*
- *Spirit Baptism and New Wineskin Fellowship*

If this is your desire, I would suggest you start with the first book listed, *The Baptism of the Holy Spirit,* and begin studying it with your prayer partner or fellowship group who participated in the 40 days of prayer and devotional study with you. You may want to invite others to join you and your group. Then individually and as a group continue to progress through each book. This will enable the Lord to strengthen the experience with Him that He has begun in your life during the past 40 days.

Or if you want to, move on to other subjects related to the baptism of the Holy Spirit. The following books that I have written could be used for individual and group study to learn about other aspects of the Spirit-baptized experience. They can be studied in any order as the Lord leads.

- *Spirit Baptism and Waiting on God*
- *Spirit Baptism and Christ's Glorious Return*

- *Spirit Baptism and Deliverance*
- *Spirit Baptism and the 1888 Message of Righteousness by Faith*
- *Spirit Baptism and Earth's Final Events*

Second, continue to pray for those on your prayer list and reach out to them. Also, add others to your list as the Lord leads, and as a group consider activities to plan to invite those on the prayer lists to attend.

Christ wants personal daily devotional study, prayer, and reaching out to others to become an integral part of every Christian's life. If this aspect of your life ends with the 40 days of prayer and devotional study, you will not grow into the fullness of Christ that He desires you to experience. Also, this is the only way to be ready for Christ's soon return. For it is the only way our intimate relationship with Christ develops and grows. May the Lord abundantly bless your continued devotional study and prayer time with Him, and your efforts to share Him with others.

Note: *All books listed are available through most Adventist Book Centers or at www.spiritbaptism.org.*

Prayer List

Name:

_____

Phone:

_____

E-mail:

_____

Address:

_____

_____

Prayer Requests:

_____

_____

_____

_____

40 Days of Prayer:

__ __ __ __ __ __ __ __ __ __

__ __ __ __ __ __ __ __ __ __

__ __ __ __ __ __ __ __ __ __

__ __ __ __ __ __ __ __ __ __

Caring Activities:

_____

_____

_____

_____

Prayer List

Name:

_____

Phone:

_____

E-mail:

_____

Address:

_____

_____

Prayer Requests:

_____

_____

_____

_____

40 Days of Prayer:

___ ___ ___ ___ ___ ___ ___ ___ ___ ___

___ ___ ___ ___ ___ ___ ___ ___ ___ ___

___ ___ ___ ___ ___ ___ ___ ___ ___ ___

___ ___ ___ ___ ___ ___ ___ ___ ___ ___

Caring Activities:

_____

_____

_____

_____

Prayer List

Name:

_____

Phone:

_____

E-mail:

_____

Address:

_____

_____

Prayer Requests:

_____

_____

_____

_____

40 Days of Prayer:

_____

_____

_____

_____

Caring Activities:

_____

_____

_____

_____

Prayer List

Name:
_____

Phone:
_____

E-mail:
_____

Address:
_____
_____

Prayer Requests:
_____
_____
_____
_____

40 Days of Prayer:
_ _ _ _ _ _ _ _ _ _
_ _ _ _ _ _ _ _ _ _
_ _ _ _ _ _ _ _ _ _
_ _ _ _ _ _ _ _ _ _

Caring Activities:
_____
_____
_____
_____

Prayer List

Name:

_____

Phone:

_____

E-mail:

_____

Address:

_____

_____

Prayer Requests:

_____

_____

_____

_____

40 Days of Prayer:

___ ___ ___ ___ ___ ___ ___ ___

___ ___ ___ ___ ___ ___ ___ ___

___ ___ ___ ___ ___ ___ ___ ___

___ ___ ___ ___ ___ ___ ___ ___

Caring Activities:

_____

_____

_____

_____

Scriptures to Claim

As you pray for these individuals every day, claim the Scriptures below on their behalf. These are taken from the *Praying Church Source Book*, pages 128, 129.

1. That God will draw them to Himself (John 6:44)

2. That they seek to know God (Acts 17:27)

3. That they believe the Word of God (1 Thess. 2:13)

4. That Satan be bound from blinding them to the truth and that his influences in their life be "cast down" (2 Cor. 4:4; 10:4, 5)

5. That the Holy Spirit work in them (John 16:8-13)

6. That they turn from sin (Acts 3:19)

7. That they believe in Christ as Savior (John 1:12)

8. That they obey Christ as Lord (Matt. 7:21)

9. That they take root and grow in Christ (Col. 2:6, 7)

Study Notes

Four Gospels. One Story.

Drawing from the perspective of each writer, Jack Blanco merges the four Gospels by tapping into the underlying harmony of each. The resulting conversational paraphrase is a down-to-earth narrative that tells the timeless, captivating story of Jesus, our Savior. Paperback, 154 pages.

3 WAYS TO SHOP

- **Visit your local Adventist Book Center®**
- **Call 1-800-765-6955**
- **Online at AdventistBookCenter.com**

Availability subject to change.

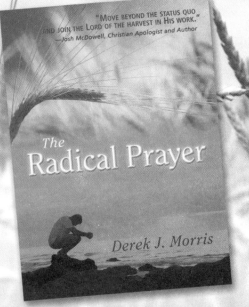